Evincepub
Publishing

Evincepub Publishing

Nehru Nagar, Bilaspur, Chhattisgarh 495001
First Published by Evincepub Publishing 2021
Copyright © Daisy Madaan 2021
All Rights Reserved.

ISBN: 978-93-90586-09-7

Price: ₹ 235/-

The Art of Baking

Homemakers to Bakers

Daisy Madaan

Contents

Foreword

This is not a cookbook or a manual of baking, if you are looking for one. No recipes, no cooking or baking tips. The book might have been titled Glorious Women Bakers rather than The Art of Baking. It is a book of inspirational stories of a few chosen successful women who have carved out for themselves a career in baking from being a housewife. Not that being a full-time housewife is less of a profession. It is a full-time job of managing home, looking after the children, the husband and the elders in the family, if you live in a joint family. There is so much work that it is simply magical that the housewife (more appropriately called a homemaker) can stretch time to additionally take up a new profession. This book is a treatise on such women.

The author has put in tremendous efforts to compile mini biographies of these miraculous women. The basic tenets of success remain the same in whichever profession you wish to excel. The top most or rather I would say the top three are hardwork, hardwork and hardwork. The others are tenacity, dedication, persistence, perseverance, honesty, fearlessness, inquisitiveness (sense of enquiry), strength and agility to remain fit and healthy under all circumstances.

Each of these women have utilized these traits to balance their duties as a housewife and their responsibility towards their profession. The stories have been woven well to keep the readers interest alive and not to degenerate into monotony. The work of each protagonist has been distinctly highlighted and sincere efforts made to differentiate each so as to make the book not putdownable but a page turner. You can read in one sitting within a couple of hours or put it on your bedside table to read one success story at a time.

The book would prove to be useful to not only people who aspire to become bakers but will inspire others also who dare to venture into different professions. In addition, it is a good read for any casual reader.

Here's wishing good luck to the author, Daisy Madaan, for a successful run of not only this book but many more to follow.

Nita Mehta

Indian celebrity chef,
author, restaurateur
and media personality

Acknowledgments

Book writing is never a one-person job. It requires cooperation and faith from people around you. I have been lucky enough to have incredibly supportive family and friends who have always motivated me to do things in the way I wished for. My heartfelt gratitude to my family – both parents and in-laws' side, and lovely friends who have helped me in each phase of book writing and provided their valuable feedback and wishes whenever I required the most.

My foremost acknowledgment to the **cake artists** and **home bakers** whose creativity and dedication motivated me to write this book. All these artists are so talented, creative and are definitely a source of inspiration for one and all.

A big thank you to the **women who are featured in this book** for sharing their personal journey with all my readers. Without your support and timely response, this book was not possible. For the last couple of months, I have been in continuous touch with these super women. All of them were very supportive and spontaneous in providing the information I was looking for. I have developed a lifelong relation with these artists. I hope their journey will stimulate many to follow their passion and succeed in their life.

I extend my gratitude to all the **reviewers** of the book. Your constant feedback and expert reviews helped me to overcome the shortcomings and release a version of the book that readers will be pleased to read.

I wish to acknowledge **Mrs. Nita Mehta**, Indian celebrity chef, author and veteran home baker who accepted my request and presented a preface for the book. Inspiring words from such a renowned person boosted my morale to release the book soon.

It will be unfair if I end this section without thanking some special people in my life.

"Life doesn't come with a manual; it comes with a mother". I give full credit for each and everything that I have gained till date to **my mother**. Her positive attitude and dedication towards family has taught me to balance work home responsibilities and face all challenges in life. She herself was an entrepreneur and successfully ran a boutique for 18 years.

It is said, "Behind every successful man there is a woman" and "Behind every successful woman there are many men".

From the day I conceived the idea of book writing, three men in my life have been playing an important role. They have guided me, and supported me in every phase of book writing.

I had a dream to become an author and this dream would not have become reality without the guidance and support of **my loving husband**. His farsightedness and ideology of thinking big has motivated me to come out of my comfort zone and complete this book. Thank you for all your directions and taking care of the kitchen and our daughter while I was interviewing people.

Since childhood, **my father** has been the most influential person in my life. He is my strength and I have always looked upon his advice whenever in distress. He has stood by me like a pillar and has taught me to be courageous and confident in every walk of life. For this book he has been the proof-reader and editor for many chapters. Thank you, 'Papa', for all the support and timely advice. Love you!

If you wish to become an engineer or doctor, you will refer to an engineer or doctor for all your queries. Similarly, for authoring this book I referred to **my brother**, who too is an author of a book titled "10 keys to attain happiness". Thank you, dear brother, for all the help and answering all my questions from the time even before I started writing this book.

Last but not the least, the book is dedicated to a beautiful angel in my life - **my daughter** who is my world. It is said that Motherhood comes with new chapters and new lessons. So, my motherhood journey is also no different. This little girl paved a way for me to explore new avenues and I moved forward following my heart and passion of writing.

A shout out for **all women** - just live your dreams. Let your dreams be the wings!!

Reviews

Being a home baker myself and having evolved in this industry in India has been an amazing experience. I could see a lot of my own journey in the stories of these amazing, enterprising women pioneers in the home baking industry, some of whom I know personally. I do believe that India is ready for a book like this which talk about the inspiring stories of women who have broken the barriers of societal and familial responsibilities to achieve tremendous success. Hats off to Daisy for having curated their stories!!

Lubna Gafoor
Sugar Artist at Buttercups, Bangalore
www.facebook.com/Buttercupscupcakes
www.instagram.com/buttercupscupcakesblr

It's interesting to learn more about famous Cake artists and Home bakers and the inspiring stories behind the names. I am sure the reader will identify with and aspire to emulate them!

Prita Dheer
Midlife Coach - researching and writing about
the Empty Nest Syndrome
www.facebook.com/DialABakercom
www.instagram.com/DialABakercom

A beautiful insight by Daisy Madaan, into the journey from being a homemaker to a home baker. Most bakers can identify with the book as it speaks about the challenges of getting started, finding support of family and friends or treading on without it, going through constant learning and adding on to their skills as one move along to the road to success. The inspiring life stories of the talented bakers in the book are a great source of motivation for homemakers who would want to follow their passion.

Hema Chhabra
Owner/Managing Director at
Fab Flavours & Fragrances P. Ltd
Managing Partner at
Apyura Premium Spreads, Delhi
www.facebook.com/FabFlavoursAndFragrances
www.instagram.com/fabflavoursandfragrances

The expert in anything was once a beginner. As the line goes this book is for the experts and this book is for the beginners. This is not only a good read but also an inspiration. Thank you for bringing out this marvel.

All the best and warm regards,
Anna Austin
Cake Canvas-happiness in a box
www.cakecanvas.in
www.facebook.com/CakeCanvasHappinessinabox
www.instagram.com/cakecanvas

'The Art of Baking - Homemakers to Bakers' is a well written and an inspirational book in which the writer has communicated success and struggle stories of passionate women in the field of baking. The writer, Daisy Madan has put a lot of effort in interviewing renowned bakers and has finally narrated it in an attractive and uniquely designed pattern to make it a quick and easy read. There are numerous beneficial snippets in the book and it's a recommended read to anyone who needs a spark of motivation to do wonders in their lives and to accept and express themselves in their respective creative fields of work.

Dr. Reema Sharma
Associate Professor in
New Horizon Engineering College,
Bangalore.

The book is really motivational. It tells us about the journey of inspirational women who have built successful businesses. It takes us to their journey from a homemaker to a successful women Entrepreneur. It's a motivational book that teaches us that we should never be afraid with one small setback. With Determination and dedication nothing is impossible. Truly enjoyed reading the book

Mrs Charanjeev Kaur
Homemaker, Hyderabad

This book is dedicated to womanhood - recounts the journey of homemakers who have made Love edible by turning into a home baker. It brings out a very powerful message of believing in your passion and that women are creators and not meant to give up their career.

The book language is lucid and written by Daisy Madan, whose journey is also inspiring as she gave up her high-flying corporate IT career and turned to Entrepreneur.

An inspiring book and will recommend to everyone who is looking for an opportunity to cash their passion.

Anchal Sardana
A Mom of two, amateur photographer is a
Senior Solution Architect with HCL, Noida

'The Art of baking- Homemakers to Bakers' by Daisy contains extremely powerful and motivational stories of the women who were homemakers earlier and are successful home bakers now.

Each story in the book is an inspiration for every woman to do something in life with the convenience of being at home.

It's a must-read for women who want to pursue their career without sacrificing much of their family time.

Shikha Gandhi Kathuria
Author of Mathemagician,
Proprietor, Bangalore.

The book shows the power of believing in oneself. All these women struggled at one point but with sheer dedication and determination they are enjoying the sweetness of success. While reading the stories of these successful women, the reader gets to think "If these women can, then I can do too". I truly believe what one of the artists in the book said, "Stepping up slowly is key to success".

Manpreet Kaur Dhillon
Homemaker and Education Assistant,
Canada

Thoughtfully written, the book talks about inspiring stories of entrepreneurs. I truly enjoyed reading the book, and highly recommend it to budding women entrepreneurs.

Neha Sharma
IT Professional, Singapore

About the Book

"She's a dreamer, a doer, a thinker. She sees possibility everywhere - "Kate Spade

"I had a dream to be a renowned artist and exhibit my paintings at international shows, but after my marriage, I couldn't continue."

"I wanted to be an entrepreneur and have my own HR consulting and management firm. However, once I had kids, all dreams shattered and now I am managing my 2 little bosses."

"I was a Branch Manager in a Bank, but had to leave the job as my husband was travelling overseas."

"I continued my freelancing content writing task after marriage but would hardly meet my deadlines due to household chores and finally I gave up."

"I was working in the corporate sector but long working hours and late-night meetings and calls were not allowing me to do justice for my home and office."

Do any of these words strike a chord with you. It may be your inner voice if you are a woman and if you are a man then this is the voice of women around you.

In both cases, my first piece of advice to you is "DO NOT WORRY". It's time to wake up and live your dreams. Certainly, it's not as easy as said, but I have a list of people and their success stories who struggled their way to achieve their dream.

This book is all about women who sacrifice their careers as at some point of time family priorities overpowers professional careers. It is often said, "Men and Women are equal" but the fact is that they are equal but not identical. We are all aware that as per biological law of nature only women can give birth and lactate. Motherhood brings its own difficulties and pushes ladies to leave their place of employment. As a tradition, it is mostly women of the house who sacrifice their profession sometimes for husband and other times for kids.

Many times, women are forced to choose between a high-flying career and a nest. The book is all about those women who being in their nest develop their talent and skills and blossom as a new identity. Woman sacrifices her career due to various reasons but that does not mean she should sacrifice her dreams. There are ways to craft your path from passion to profession. Many have proved that their passion and skills have given them new directions and success. If they can do it, you can also.

WOMANHOOD

Naari kal bhi bhari thi, naari aaj bhi bhaari hai!!

Purush kal bhi abhari tha, purush aaj bhi abhaari hai!!

नारी कल भी भारी थी नारी आज भी भारी हैं,

पुरुष कल भी आभारी था पुरुष आज भी आभारी हैं।

Woman, beautiful creation of God! Woman who is considered as full of love in whatever role she plays - daughter, sister, wife, mother!

All women are unique in their way, so do men! Whenever the word women come to mind, we get a picture of a soft and sleek human being. But in reality, a woman is very strong internally who is born to sacrifice, appreciate, care and love her family from the bottom of her heart.

Women of the 21st century are cheerful, overflowing, daring and goal-oriented, they just don't sit tight for approval. Present time women are allowed to communicate and execute their choices. Today's women are the women of the future!

It is said that man and woman are two pillars of any house. While a man is considered physically strong, but real strength is the woman of the house. Without a woman, life is fragmented. She easily oversees and sorts out the whole world around her, she shapes our lives and gives it an importance! Being a woman in itself is a gift, and we should praise womanhood with a great deal of energy and abundance to remind all the ladies around the globe about their significance and qualities in our lives.

Women are like onions with multiple layers of roles, responsibilities and capabilities. Keep unfolding the layers and keep admiring the beauty and strength that lies within.

There are many sectors which are women oriented and they have done wonders. One such profession is of Home Bakery. To fulfill the appetite needs of kids and family members, women who are passionate about cooking, start their experiments in the kitchen with different ingredients and soon find their true calling as baking. It is then when Home Maker turns Home Baker.

It is rightly said, where there is a whisk there is a way and these home bakers are making love edible at home by their passion of baking.

The Baking Industry

Cakes have been there for centuries. With the advancement of technology and customization in every product around, products are designed in such ways that they create memories for years to come. Globalization has led to change in eating habits of Indians and inclination towards baking products. Cake cutting ceremony is now not limited to special occasions of Weddings and Birthdays. Cakes are also ordered on other special occasions like Baby Shower, Anniversaries, Graduation, Mother's Day, Father's Day, Valentine's Day. Cake lovers even order cakes every month celebrating the monthly Birthdays of new born babies, although the baby cannot eat cake at that stage.

Till late 90s and even in early 20s, especially in India spending money on a lavish Wedding or Birthday Cake was not so common. Though the wedding budget used to be a big amount, people hardly paid out money for edible things. The mindset of people was that they were more pleased and satisfied in investing in Gold and silk sarees.

After the internet and social media came into existence there has been a huge boom in the customer base of Baking products. Designer cake has become part and parcel Of every special occasion. In fact, before the actual treat, Cake acts as a visual treat for all. With the demand for cakes and other baked products increasing, the baking industry has flourished by leaps and bounds in the last decade. Not only traditional bakeries and hotels, but individuals are putting their heart and soul in trying out new recipes and coming out with creative designs.

Home bakery is a common entrepreneurial endeavor trend these days. Home baking has consistently been a well-known pursuit, however with new technological developments people have been capable of monetizing their talent and creativity. Many Home Bakers are getting international artists' attention as they have zeal to work for their passion. Home Baker's creativity and innovations are setting new trends and are inspiring many to follow the same path. Both bakers and customers are not compromising on the average looking cakes.

There have been days in the past when many would have hardly thought that home bakery or cake artists would be a new profession. Some common dialogs that many aspiring home bakers might have listened to in their life, *"Cake to bana leti ho, kaam kya karti ho?"*, *"Cake banane ke bhi itni paise milte hain?"*, etc.

But now, many of you will agree with me that Home Bakers are the real talent. Home bakers create their own opportunities with their design, creativity and new flavors. COVID-19 pandemic had hit the lifestyle of many and had brought a boom in home bakery business. Home bakers are preferred for customization, taste, hygiene and convenience. People avoided going out and chose home bakers to curb their hunger and taste needs.

Indian Women are blessed with special characteristics. They will try to manage with whatever is available for them and have taken Baking industry to such a level that now we are competing with different countries. If you have real talent in baking, then there are endless opportunities for home Bakers.

The book is an effort to inspire every woman out there to find their passion and excel in that so that you become a role model for one and all.

Challenges faced by Home Bakers

"Challenges are what make life interesting; overcoming them is what makes life meaningful" - Joshua J. Marine

Every entrepreneurship has its own highs and lows. Nothing comes easy and is simple. Home based business is a good option for women who have to look after kids and home and also aspire to have their own identity. Home baking has become trendy business now-a-days. The creativity of bakers has won the hearts of millions. While there are masses who admire the creativity and talent of this business, still there are many who consider this as an ordinary profession with not much potential.

The intent of this chapter is definitely not to demotivate upcoming home bakers from venturing this business, but to prepare you well before you start looking into an opportunity to adopt it. If we know beforehand what challenge we are going to face, we can gear up our girds well in time and face it to defeat it.

So, before we read about the journey of home bakers who have gained name and fame working in this industry, I would like to highlight a few challenges which I presume every home baker might have faced during their journey.

1. Tremendous Creativity:

The present trend is of personalization. The digital world has made customization reach to its epitome - from personal commodities like towels, pillows, T-shirts etc. to toys, or even office accessories like pens, paperweights, diaries - you name it and it is customizable. Cakes are no exception in this category. Customization opens the door of creativity and so bakers have to be very creative in their designs and presentations. There are a few exceptions that have survived with their old school designs. But, to compete with the best, you have to channelize your potential into making the designs extraordinary.

2. Variety in every order:

Customers not only ask for personalization, but they also look for different flavors and designs every time they order a cake. While talking to different bakers, we found out that customers will just download pictures from the internet and ask for the same design. Many times, design does not go well with the flavor they chose and other times particular design could be made only for a particular size. Few customers want flavor out of the world. So, a baker has to come up with all possible designs and flavors to meet the customer expectations.

3. Geographical expansion is limited:

Geographical location can be a great challenge in this sector. While some things are available all across the world, you cannot expect a home baker to deliver to some other faraway state. However, some bakers and cake artists are successful in delivering their cakes across state or country boundaries with extra care and precautions.

4. Adopting of unfit pricing model:

Pricing is a very vibrant, tricky and thoughtful process. Sometimes, home Bakers keep low prices just to gain confidence and get customers. This is not the right strategy to consider. Home Baking is just like any other business and it should always be profitable.

5. Customers expect Home Bakers to give cakes at lesser prices than bakeries:

Bakeries usually employ labor at a cheap cost and that makes the profit margins very high for them. While home bakers toil away, doing most work on their own, they are not regarded as much. Rather, they are expected to give cakes at even lower prices. While interviewing experts of this industry, it is always recommended by one and all that every baker should value their art and never degrade yourself.

6. Continuous learning and upgrading your skills else you will be stagnant:

In this ever-changing world, it is very important to always update yourself with the new. No matter how hard you try, it is cumbersome to keep up with the prevailing trend. Hence, learning and upgrading becomes an essential part of baking. Never feel shy to learn.

7. Unbeatable zeal is important:

A lot of hard work is required. Whatever is seen on Facebook or Instagram seems very lucrative and fancy but only a baker knows what he or she has put in to get the required result. It may encompass a lot of wastage of resources that cannot be used up later. Or in another case, it may be that the design is very demanding with respect to the money being paid. There are a lot of reasons which might result in your motivation going down. Decide not to pay attention to the things which bring you down and achieve your dream of being the best baker.

8. Create a piece of art and know how to sell it:

Home bakers should be good at creativity and have adequate managerial skills to make profits. While it goes without saying that hard work and creativity is important, having a business mindset is also essential. You have to take care of the monetary aspects of your business; this does not necessarily mean knowing where to spend. But, how much ingredients to buy in your budget, calculating the price to be paid by the customer, focusing on making profits along with making profits.

9. Home delivery:

Delivering straight to the homes of customers is an added service that is taken for granted. Sometimes, it is difficult to leave the home and other times, you are not aware of the location that the customer has requested for the cake to be delivered. There could be a myriad of reasons which makes it so challenging. Even if you hire a person for delivery, their charges are not counted and free home delivery is expected.

10. Material not available and imported from different countries.

There could be times when everything is perfect, the customer is paying a handsome amount, the area to be delivered is nearby and the design is also doable, but a particular product that is used for baking is out of stock. It is highly troublesome in such cases. Unavailability of ingredients either due to being out of stock or not being available in the country lowers your motivation and chances to earn.

11. Undue requirements by some customers:

It might happen for instance, that a customer wants exactly the face of their pet on a cake with the same amount of whiskers and the same color of eyes and all they send you is a picture of the pet. It becomes very difficult to keep up with the expectations laid out by the customer. Even if you live up to their expectations, there is always going to be some flaw that they will find.

12. Educating clients and making customers understand new things in the market:

Helping and educating customers into deciding what designs to choose for a cake and coming up with modifications in these is another factor to be taken into consideration. For instance, if a customer wants a pineapple cake and you suggest a blueberry cheesecake instead, they might not necessarily want that. You must help them be aware of the potential problems you may face like unavailability of seasonal fruits during that time.

These are general challenges that most home bakers have experienced or will experience during their journey of baking. With your dedication and hard work, you can easily overcome them and be successful like superwoman in the chapters to follow.

———❧———

Inspiring Stories of Successful Home Bakers and Cake Artists

Tina Scott Parashar

Top 10 cake artists in India

First Indian Brand Ambassador for various
International brands

Founder and Editor at
Incredible India CAKE Magazine

Official Representative for
Cake International for India

"In whatever you do, you're not going to stand out unless you think big and have ideas that are truly original. That comes from tapping into your own creativity, not obsessing over what everyone else is doing." —Sophia Amoruso, founder of Nasty Gal

The success story of any successful Entrepreneur or Bollywood celebrity is motivating only if they have stood out of the crowd and have become victorious in whatever they did. Their farsightedness and imaginative vision have inspired many to follow the same path. The above quote holds true for Tina Scott Parashar who started just nine years back with baking a cake at home for her son, further enhanced her skills in decorating cakes, participated in various competitions followed by judging multiple cake shows, organizing different collaborations and now editor and founder of Incredible India Cake Magazine. Her exemplary innovations and efforts to unite people from different countries under one umbrella has opened opportunities for many in the same industry.

The global industry has completely transformed over the years and the kind of creations we see these days are absolutely mind boggling. Women who are passionate have raised the standards of this industry altogether to a new level. The home baking business is no longer restricted to Birthday and celebration cakes. If you are an aspiring or an established home baker, do not forget the baking industry is like an ocean and you can fish as much as you can.

One can bake from traditional cakes to designer cakes, fancy floral cakes to multi-tier wedding cakes but baking life-size sculptures is unique in itself. In 2019, Tina had created a life-size welcome display at the main entrance of Cake International, Birmingham (the biggest cake shows in the world). It was called the Incredible Indian Welcome display and consisted of several life-size cakes displaying the rich cultural heritage of India. The team of seven artists who were the best-known names in the global cake community was led by Tina Scott Parashar.

The Expert in anything was once a beginner

Tina has worked in a corporate media house for six years. She decided to quit her job when her son was born to focus on her family and the timing was fortuitous as it led her to explore her passion for cake decoration. It is at this time that she decided to pursue the art of cake decorating. As her son grew older, she decided to make cake for his son's second birthday on her own. To start with she did a couple of introductory classes to understand the basics of baking and cake decorating as she had no prior experience in this field. This is a profession which requires you to constantly upgrade your skills if you want to grow as a professional. You can decide to stick with the basics if you want to keep it as a casual hobby, but if you want to excel, you need appropriate training and practice. Over the years, she spent a lot of time honing her skills and practicing.

Unfolding a journey to success

As she kept decorating cakes, she entered into competitions including in South Africa, where she lived and then Cake International, UK. She then improved her skills and entered global competitions, where she got the opportunity to meet and attend classes from some of the best names in the industry. As in any profession, it takes hours and hours of practice to improve on your own and to get details right.

Her excellence and practice have made her achieve which is well deserved for her. For any baker any one of the achievements is a matter of pride, but Tina has a long list to be proud of: -

1. She has been rewarded as Top 10 Indian Cake artists by Cake Masters Magazine, UK consecutively in 2017 and 2018. This program recognizes the top talent in the baking industry across the globe and awards the best cake decoration and sugarcraft talent every year.

2. She has won Gold in events organized by Cake International in London in 2015 and Gold and second place in Cake International in Birmingham, 2016.

3. The first award that she earned was in the year 2014. It was a Gold award for the World Orchid Conference.

4. She has another feather in her cap for being the Cake masters UK finalist for best collaboration.

Judge in multiple competition

As stated above, Tina started baking cakes at her home for her personal occasions, and participated and won different competitions. She has made all kinds of cakes but what she loves doing most is making life-size cake sculptures as well as cake busts and figurines. Her achievements are not limited to baking and winning in various competitions. She is Official Representative for Cake International for India and judge in various National and International cake shows. Some shows are listed as follows:

1. Judge for the Indian Cake Awards.

2. She has also been asked to judge several international competitions including the ones for Cakeflix by Paul Bradford, Serdar Yener's pastillage competition, India's Top 100 bakers and Saracino international competitions.

3. She was invited to Poland to be a member of the Jury Board of Polish Cake Designers Championship In 2019 by Expo Sweet, Poland.

She believes the key to win competition is to always practice well and learn new skills to make yourself better than the best. She further explains that participating in global competitions and collaborating with other global artists can expand your creativity and showcase your talent to masses. Without doing this, you run the risk of being repetitive, one dimensional and confined to your own shell. If you have a desire to be followed instead of being a follower, break your limits and explore the various opportunities that you can seek through competitions and collaborations.

Challenge your Limits

"Every challenge you face today makes you stronger tomorrow. The challenge of life is intended to make you better, not bitter." — **Roy T. Bennett**

Challenges make you more responsible. Always remember no one can achieve any success without any struggle. Any story becomes a success story only when it reveals the challenges faced by the concerned person. There is no doubt that life is interesting because of the challenges faced and becomes meaningful with the courage to overcome those difficult times.

Tina Scott Parashar feels being a cake artist is extremely time intensive passion and requires a tremendous amount of attention to detail. The amount of hours she needs to put in while participating or organizing contests or being a judge in various competitions keeps her away from her family for an extended period of time. So managing relations with work really becomes a challenge at times. To overcome such challenges, she tries to spend maximum time with family whenever time permits.

The next obstacle that she states is to continuously upgrade your skills and produce new and inspiring work to showcase your talent. Enhancing your artistry is essential for sustaining the old clients and attracting new ones.

She, too, faced many challenges especially when she entered her cakes in international competitions. But, for her, every competition has been a learning opportunity where she had learned from her mistakes and feedback from the judges. She has never looked at these or any other instances as failures, but an opportunity to learn from them and improve herself and her skill set. One with such attitude in life is bound to succeed and move forward and excel in whatever he or she does.

Advice for upcoming entrepreneurs:

The people with the Best Advice are usually the ones who have been through the most. Ms Tina is the first Indian to be chosen as a brand ambassador for various international brands in the industry. She has her forum Incredible India Cake magazine community that provides recipes and tutorials for skill building from some of the best global artists in the industry. This is a free platform for any artists who wish to join. Home Bakers who have used the platform have provided fantastic reviews. The feedback and comments from bakers around the world has helped the community to grow quickly. So, if you want to learn the basics or advance things in Baking, do join this forum and get updated yourself with the latest recipes and techniques from the experts.

Since Ms Tina has experienced this industry and has been in communication with cake artists all over the world, she holds the opinion that the future of this industry is very bright especially in the country like India where new talent is born every day. The industry has grown rapidly in our country with many new artists coming up. Indian artists are getting opportunities which were not available previously. The availability of tools and materials for the craft have also improved tremendously compared to when she started. There is a lot of exciting new work being put up by Indian artists these days.

She also led a separate Indian artist Zone for Cake International Virtual Edition this year showcasing the works of some of the best Indian artists. There are a lot more opportunities now than ever before. So this is the golden period to start or fast-forward your journey.

The expert always emphasizes on to start with the basics. Make sure you practice well to get the details right before you venture into competitions. Learn to take constructive criticism and use it to improve your skills rather than feel disheartened by it as there is immense talent in this industry. This is an art where you can devote as much time and energy as you can spare. The rewards are commiserate to the amount of effort you put in. For artists, it is now much easier to showcase your work, your talent and skill to the global community and earn recognition and grow your brand.

Compliments from Clients:

"It looked so lifelike. The work that must have gone into the cake and then the art work, I applaud you. You did a fantastic job. Congratulations "

"Fabulous Tina, you were a joy to work with and the team working together, the Feature was outstanding. How do we top that? You really did Cake International proud."

"Your life-size cake has gone viral! I have received it as a message on various WhatsApp groups and Facebook forwards. You made Indians proud everywhere! Thank you for representing our country on an international platform".

She is the founder of The Incredible India Cake Magazine Community on Facebook and in just a few months it has grown to a large community. The main intent behind this platform, is to bring together Indian artists as well as several international globally renowned artists into the same platform. The group has several tutorials, videos, recipes to help home bakers and upcoming artists every week. As of January 2021, the group has crossed 33K members in a short span of ten months.

Tina considers her role as promoting and developing Indian talent rather than seeing them as competition. She also promotes Indian talent in her role as the official ambassador for Cake International for India. So if you are someone who has either just started your journey in the baking industry or already an expert but not aware of this community, do join and get connected with the best talent of the world. Tina is doing a fabulous job in promoting Indian Talent, so why not avail an opportunity by joining her community. We congratulate her and wish her all the good luck for the work she is doing to highlight Indian talent.

Contact Details: +971 50 729 9140

Facebook page:

https://www.facebook.com/TinaScottParasharsCakeDesign

Instagram page:

https://www.instagram.com/incredibleindiacakemagazie

Ila Prakash Singh

Awarded the Best Home Baker of Gurugram

Ex Chef at Windsor Manor Sheraton

Handled Hotel Operations at Chola Sheraton

Deputy Sales Manager at Taj Bengal

"You don't have to love cooking to cook, but you have to do more than love baking to bake. You have to bake out of love"- Com Junod.

Every entrepreneur mentions the challenging phase they have come across while starting their career, and often their stories start with something beyond imagination. Like everyone, you must be wondering the genuinity behind the struggle that has been mentioned in the report as it sounds baseless. Still, this hero will take you to a new horizon, a special session for all those beautiful middle-aged ladies whose personal life demands the sacrifice of her career. What would you have done if you had kids at home and the job required indecent working hours! Quit is the only remedy that comes across, but these 48 years young, optimistic, energetic, fun-loving home baker will change your outlook! After working for ten years in renowned hotels, in the hospitality industry, she now runs her successful business from her home in Gurugram!!

She truly defines the reason why women are said to be the best creativity by God. Read more about her to get acquainted with this fact:

Why did she choose to be a home baker?

Ila Prakash Singh completed her hotel management graduation from Welcomgroup Graduate School of Hotel Administration (WGSHA) in Manipal in 1995 and her splendid experience in the hospitality industry makes her best fit for this business. She was in charge of the bakery and buffet desserts in Windsor Manor Sheraton, so she specialized in baking and confectionery. Baking bread for the buffet was a regular routine for her. She confesses that a chef's job is never easy because as a trainee no one teaches you. It is learnt on the job by doing small odd jobs helping the senior chefs gradually learning the tricks of the trade. It also depends on your interest and willingness to grasp the method, dedication, sincerity, experiment with different ingredients and create new recipes.

When she started her job in the hospitality Industry, fewer women were seen in hotel cookhouses. The fresher graduates were considered a threat to existing staff. The money earned was small, and the job position was on contract, but with her conviction and dedication, she managed to lead in different kitchens during her tenure there. She was always a replacement for any senior chef going on leave thus giving her the opportunity to handle the particular kitchen single-handedly leading to her rich knowledge of various cuisines.

It was not easy to start from scratch after she took a sabbatical for almost four years, but yes, she made it! The idea of being a chef and home-baker came as she wanted to be at home with her kids(twins) who were two and a half years old then. Baking was a part of her profession while she had worked with Windsor Manor Sheraton, Bangalore. She combined her ambition and desire to get back to work with her baking and sales and marketing experiences under the name of Truffle Tangles in Gurugram back in 2008.

Motherhood is bliss! After her twins were born, she preferred to stay at home to take care of her kids. Like every mother, she enjoyed the blissful moments of seeing her babies grow in front of her eyes. She unfolds how those moments are most precious when you see your baby crawl for the first time, turn for the first time. Those baby steps, falling after a few steps, and then getting up to try to walk again is a matter of pride and prize for any mother on this earth.

 After trying her hands on multiple multi-level marketing and other things, she realized that those were not her cup of tea as a full-time profession. She was wondering what could be that particular profession that can act like her soul food, but her journey as a baker was not a bed of roses.

 Individual pages in everyone's life take them to the height of success. This chef turned home baker also had several real-time episodes that had taught her a lot!

Bitter experiences - lessons to be learned!!

Every experience makes you grow and excel in your business. When you are into an industry which involves dealing with different types of people, then every dealing will be a unique experience in itself and it is a hard fact of life that all experiences are not always good. Lessons learned when you confront the difficult times make you evolve into a strong and better person. In her tenure of thirteen years, she too did face difficult times dealing with customers and failures in order getting delivered in ignorance. We not only learn from our own experience, but stories from successful people are also an inspiration, the level of Ila is one such kind. So hereby some moments shared which she took as an opportunity to develop herself.

Real Life Episode 1

A person ordered food for the party with some advance amount. The food included cakes, cupcakes, two main dishes, rice variety, etc. Ila's supportive husband delivered the food at the said residence, and the customer paid a partial amount. The same person came to their home after a couple of days and again made the partial payment as he fell short of cash. He promised to pay the remaining by net banking after reaching his home. After two days, Ila called him to remind him of the remaining amount; he said if she wanted the money, she would need to collect the remaining money from a particular hotel.

She is blessed with several distinctive qualities, and patience is the biggest asset that has won her standard to this level. Bitter and such weird experiences had never stopped her from moving towards her goal.

Real Life Episode 2

A wife ordered a special surprise cake for her husband on the occasion of their wedding anniversary. When the cake was delivered to their residence, since the husband was not aware that any such cake was ordered, he got annoyed and ended with arguments with the wife to order such a costly cake. The payment was made for the cake but what followed was worse. He posted lousy comments about her on social media groups as if she had looted them.

She never came up with any inadequate words for the client, and that won the heart of all; instead, she just posted her work in return as she knew it is the work that matters the most!

There were times when she cooked meals for her clients, but they never reverted to pick up or to pay for her hard work but still, she continued her career as she believed that these were the challenges for which she needed to prepare her mind.

Some of the extraordinary qualities she is blessed with, which makes her a successful entrepreneur, are listed here.

Qualities like hard work, strong foundation, energy, risk-bearing capacity, honest, service-oriented, and fairways to do business, and many such things make what she is today! Mind it, these qualities are necessary ingredients for any business and are not limited to Baking.

Look into the mirror, that's your competition.

There is a famous quote by Daylle Deanna Schwartz, "When you're really good. No one is competition. No one". Ila's confidence and strengths make her unique among home bakers. She holds the opinion that most of the home bakers are doing good and every home baker cannot bake everything. Each has a specialized niche, own strengths, capacities and support system, so there is no point in competing with other home bakers. Her knowledge, experience and practice to handle people while working in the hospitality industry strengthens her attitude while working in service-oriented business. In a nutshell she was and hardly is bothered about competition.

She always believes in a well-known saying, "My only competition is with the person that I was yesterday" and every day strives to make herself better and focused on whatever she can offer and cater to. In the quest to compete with herself, she did more than her capacity. She proudly says that whatever she did, it was not because the competition was doing it, but she did it for herself and made herself better.

Achievements and Specializations:

Ila Prakash Singh has been awarded as the winner in the category of Home-Based Bakers in 2018 as per people's choice hosted by the Gurgaon Foodie Facebook group. Before winning the title, she had been runner-up for four consecutive years.

She states that for the last four years, during the winter and Christmas season her European Plum cake which contains eighteen types of nuts soaked in whiskey, rum, and brandy has become hot selling. It has a fridge life of one year and outside it can be consumed any time during winters. In the year 2020, she broke all her previous year's records and sold more than 400 plum cakes in the season.

She specializes in Chocolate truffle which contains no butter, no cream and can be consumed as an after-dinner dessert. This cake with egg has a shelf life of ten days and even more. She realized its shelf life with a funny experience. Once a person from Gurugram ordered a cake for his wife on Valentines. The client didn't show up as he travelled to Mumbai and every other alternative day he would get in touch with Ila and assured her that he was coming soon to pick up the cake. Since he was in regular conversation, she did not deliver the cake to any other customer and finally, after twenty-one days she cut the cake at her home to check if the cake was fine. She was not so surprised when the cake tasted perfect even after so many days.

Apart from the above, Red velvet (cream cheese) and fruit cake prepared by her are in great demand. If you order one kg fruit cake with her, it will come to one and half finally as the quantity of fruits is really substantial.

She also has an art of mixing and matching different flavors, so the final result is altogether a different cake. With her innovation and gut feeling she made red velvet with truffle which is a unique combination and hardly people try out such combinations. (Of Course, soon other bakers had introduced red velvet with truffles too). She also feels delighted when she gets appreciation from her clients for her interesting creations of red velvet black forest which is composed of red velvet sponge, cream cheese, truffle and cherries.

Smooth seas do not make a skillful sailor

"You learn something valuable from all of the significant events and people, but you never touch your true potential until you challenge yourself to go beyond imposed limitations."

— Roy T. Bennett

Ila has challenged herself many times. She started her journey single-handedly when her twin sons were two and half years old. In her initial days, starting from creating to printing and distributing the pamphlets, preparing and delivering the food, she has done it all by herself. She recalls that she often used to have multiple trips to the car as she used to carry one of her kids with food in another hand and settled him in the car and then fetch the second kid from home to car. While she drives to deliver food, the kids used to sleep in the car, and while coming back again, she used to have double trips to her home as carrying sleeping kids together was not possible.

She is a one-man army when it comes to purchasing, accepting orders, designing, baking, icing, preparing food, packing, delivering, cleaning the kitchen. She giggles and remarks that her sons also offer their help in packing, but sometimes it is willingly, and other times it is unwillingly done. They are very supportive and provide a helping hand when she sets up stalls during different events.

She remarks that the real challenge is when multiple customers are calling at the same time. This is a common situation in every homemaker and home bakers' life when mobile, intercom, doorbells are ringing simultaneously. To add to that, nowadays we have WhatsApp chats, calls, Facebook chats, telegram, signal, video calls with multiple customers - all happening within a few minutes. Unnerving moments!

How pandemic affected her business?

On March 24th, 2020, when Mr Narendra Modi, Prime Minister of India called the nationwide lockdown due to the ongoing Covid-19 pandemic. All hotels, restaurants and eating joints were closed to avoid the spread of the disease. While many explored and developed their cooking skills during that time, still there were others who were craving for outsourced food. Realizing customer's needs and constant requests from existing clients stimulated Ila to expand her menu to savory sections too. With a curfew pass she was able to cater to Gurugram. Her husband delivered all the orders outside her apartment complex taking all precautions. Now she is catering orders for pizzas, patties, burgers, chicken rolls, breads, specialty foods and other savories. While she giggles, she revealed that she had not cooked and catered so much as she did during this time. Clients are so fond of her cooking and dishes, that whether there is any occasion or not, they will order food from her.

Compliments from Clients:

"Meeting Ila and tasting her cake and chocolates made me feel that the delicacy was a combination of real talent, love, professionalism, and passion altogether. Have not eaten such wonderful chocolates that were specially prepared for us till morning 4 A.M. I can still feel the taste and see the loving expression on Ila's face which was of complete satisfaction since every person in the meet of 40 people were relishing it. I am a big fan of your cakes and chocolate, but I have become a big fan of yours before that. Love you loads. Keep spreading sweetness."

"Shout out to TT for coming in on short notice for my fiancée's birthday. I ordered a 1 kg chocolate truffle cake with some vague design themes, and they provided something way better than expected. The taste was fantastic, (without butter, even) and we demolished it in minutes. Prepped in time, tasted fantastic, reasonably priced and looked incredible, and made me score a lot of brownie points. Couldn't recommend more to anyone else in Gurgaon looking for designer cakes. Thanks, Ila."

"As I said earlier, I was waiting for the last two years to order a special cake from you, and though the wait was worth it, I truly wish the next wait is shorter than two years. Your cake was even better than the reference image I gave you and it was fun for everyone. The sweetness, moistness, and flavor were what bowled

everyone over. We have almost devoured it in one go and barely managed to save a few slices for the next day. Kids loved it, and I couldn't have wished for anything better. Thank you so much for such a beautiful cake. You stand tall for your reputation in GF, and you deserve all the admiration and praise."

Ila Prakash Singh is a wonder woman and an inspiration for all those women who have to sacrifice their career for their family. She with her strong determination and will power is an example for many who just sit and complain about the adverse situation they face. She gives full credit of her success to the training and discipline that she inculcated while working in different hotels. She was the only woman amongst all men while she worked at Windsor Manor Sheraton. Her exemplary entrepreneur journey is merely a result of churning out long demanding hours in the kitchen to get perfection in all spheres. She never shies off to give honest recommendations to her customers which retains customers' confidence and trust on her. If you are in Gurugram or NCR region, get connected with her and fulfill your starving needs with the yummylicious baked items that she offers. She delivers dry cakes, brownies, plum cakes, and chocolates across India.

Contact Details: +91 9818227512

Facebook page: https://www.facebook.com/Truffletangles/

Instagram page: https://www.instagram.com/truffletanglesbyila

Twitter Handle: https://twitter.com/TruffleTangles

LinkedIn: https://www.linkedin.com/in/ilaprakashsingh36/

Website: www.truffletangles.com

Ashwini Sarabhai

Software Engineer, India's Top 10 cake artist,
Cake Oscars Finalist,
Judge in multiple Cake Shows
ICES Approved Teacher

"If baking is any labor at all, it's a labor of love. A love that gets passed from generation to generation" - Regina Brett

The notion of the youth yearning to grab every career opportunity that seems promising has existed for a while. There seems like a trend in career choices rapidly replenishing itself every decade. The 90s were no different; it was the time of striving to become a doctor or an engineer. Ashwani was one of the academically intelligent students and successfully earned a degree in engineering. It followed by a job at an IT company and achieved what seemed to be a distant dream for many. Despite the major slumps in the sector in around 2001 and 2008, she continued to thrive.

You must be wondering why I switched the narrative from baking to the engineering or the IT industry. It is not because of my education in engineering that draws me to share the story of Ashwani; the persistent hustle portrayed by this prodigious woman does.

Ashwini Sarabhai was born and raised in the beautiful city of Mumbai. After completing her education, she embarked on a professional journey with Infosys. She worked on numerous projects and included one of them in the US. During her stay there, she enrolled herself in various prestigious baking courses. This bird had taken a flight and did not look back since.

Starting by taking a few orders from her acquaintances in the US, she also started to impart knowledge about baking to whoever wished to learn. After returning to India, her business expanded to Pune and then Hyderabad.

Home baking businesses generally are considered to be constrained in terms of location. The switch of the city implies creating new clientele, exploring places to get ingredients, etc.

India's First Online Cake Making Courses

Ashwini has a degree in engineering and integrated her knowledge of baking with technology. Altruistic as she is, she introduced the concept of cake making courses in India. It allowed home bakers and artists to learn the art of baking, without having to step out. That too, at an economical cost.

The Greek philosopher Aristotle once said, "Those who know do, those that understand teach." She did not keep the techniques that made her baking extraordinary a secret. She believes in the ideology of passing on the knowledge.

She understands the importance of practice, creativity, and experience. While speaking to her, Ashwini recollects that she started her online classes once she had mastered the skill. She did not want to preach while being as naive as a half-baked cake.

The classes and workshops that she conducts are known for the delivery method with a friendly charisma. She explains the smallest of the details of the ingredients and design cheerfully. Her students gracefully remarked while putting forward even the basic questions without hesitating. She acknowledges the smallest of queries like the usage of baking soda, the purpose of baking powder, the difference between these two common ingredients, etc.

She has been sharing her knowledge in an online mode for over a decade now. She has trained thousands of home bakers and artists across the globe. Her Live sessions and workshops have classes for all categories - baking, filling, frosting, decorative art. But, she specializes in sugar flower sculpting and conducts multiple batches to teach this skill as well. Depending upon the expertise of a learner, there is a different set of classes for each.

Anyone who wishes to learn has the flexibility to choose from individual and group sessions. During these live workshops, students experience the demonstration of the way it takes place. If learners are unable to attend the live sessions, they may purchase the pre-recorded lectures.

Critiquing is an Art

The eye for detail makes her a competent judge of baking competitions across the globe. Indian Cake Awards (ICA), International online cake competition ByBora are two of the many she has judged. According to her, the devotion that goes into producing art is unparalleled. And, to cross paths with artists with varied cultures and different thought processes, she finds herself in a state of awe.

The rules and categories for every event is different set by the organizer. Most likely, there are different categories like decorative exhibits, tasting buds, etc. On the other hand, the online competitions include the design perspective and aesthetic aspect because of the inability to conduct tasting judgment. These contests are in accord with the expertise of the participants. Every participant is the best judge for themselves and decides the level they want to enroll. A lot of times realization dawns after the experience.

Ashwini has a few aces up her sleeve to be able to judge cakes appropriately. The four rules that she swears by are below:

1. The first step is to critically evaluate the creativity put in for the appearance of the cake. After it resonates in terms of appeal, dig deeper into detailed aesthetics like color and theme.

2. Since every competition bears a different set of rules, it is to the judge to see that all of them are acknowledged.

3. Innovation and the ideology behind the creation is another factor to be considered. Out of the box thinking and interpretation of the theme makes or mar the contestant's winning stance.

4. The neatness of the product is crucial. Be it a minimalistic or complex cake - precision turns it beautiful.

Price your Art Well

In any business, pricing strategy is the toughest and yet, an important aspect. High prices imply a reduction in sales whereas, low prices affect the profit margins. Low prices also tend to be thought of as decreased quality. An optimum price constitutes all your costs and profit margins while attracting customers. Some factors that affect pricing include:

1. **Geographic location** - Ingredients, utensils, staff, and other essentials are not readily available at all locations. A baker's effort to cross these barriers must be of regard.

2. **Category of the product** - Luxe, delicacy or everyday products. To be able to decide the price according to each is an important decision.

3. **Infrastructure costs** - Infrastructure includes charges for setup, electricity, water, team size, packaging, and delivery charges.

4. **Experience of the baker** - It takes a sufficient amount of time in the field to be able to gauge all the factors for deciding the pricing. The clientele, faith, and trust, builds over time.

Richie Norton, a renowned business coach, speaker, and author always emphasizes pricing. He has a quote, "Dear entrepreneurs: Pricing is branding. Branding is a mindset. Your mindset, not the market, determines how much money you make or don't make. Think about that"

Ashwini holds a similar mindset and suggests, "Let no one decide your worth for you. Be aware of the inner call and value your time and experience. Set profit margins as repayment to yourself for your toiling. Adjusting prices according to the market price is a bad decision. The market is big and readily pays for the good quality."

She further adds, "In a densely populated country like India, you should focus on catering to a specific kind of audience. If you start feeling insecure in the pursuit to cater to all kinds of audiences, you are likely to get trapped in the rat race and minimize the prices. The peace of mind and satisfaction for getting the right price for the effort contribute to the business. At times the pricing model is appropriate but business strategies are not. Your wit and talent in getting things organized strategically act as the backbone of the profits of a business."

Take every opportunity as a challenge

Ashwini started her baking endeavor at a time when the industry was yet to flourish. Working on all fronts and dealing with the low availability of ingredients and materials. Most of the stock had to get imported. Basic materials like fondant were also scarce. Awareness among people was less as they were reluctant to spend on edibles. During those times, people had the mentality to compare spending on cakes and buying a saree or investing in gold. She strived gigantically to spread awareness among people to invest in a cake.

Recruiting staff was another hurdle as only a few people knew the baking skills. Training them from scratch and a lot of times, people left after that. In the present times, too, there is a similar pattern. But trained workers are not scarce. It makes the replacement of staff not as big of an issue.

Ashwini admits her journey gave her an abundance of knowledge and made her stronger. It taught her to take adversities in the face of it and be resilient. She recalls the times when there was a shortage of fondant due to a sudden pause in import. She did not let this be a digression from delivering the orders. She could make fondant herself and was able to please her clients well with the cakes they desired. Her positive approach towards life and profession blossomed her into a victorious person both in professional and personal lives. With sheer dedication and hard work, she came out with a product - **'ShineLine.'** It is versatile in accord with the clients' demand - cakes embellished with gold and intricate designs in dazzling metallic colors.

She credits her success to the support of her family. She feels grateful to the almighty for the doting parents, a loving husband, and affectionate in-laws. Apart from that, her young children have also been a helping hand to her in this venture. Inspired by their artist mother, they started their YouTube channel of the baking genre. During summer breaks, they invite friends willing to learn the skills. Ms. Sarabhai giggles when she mentions how she adores and appreciates them for teaching so patiently.

The saga of the cake that made a bride cry

During the wedding of a notable man's daughter (Identity not disclosed), Ashwini was hired to prepare the cake. The big fat Indian wedding reception took place in a luxurious hotel. She decided to deliver the five-tier cake on her own. The cake went through several security checks and scanning. The hotel staff that carried the cake made an erroneous fiasco when he decided to tilt it significantly with the intent of holding it better. The baker, the bride, and several others around witnessed the havoc. By the time anyone could guide him on, it was too late. It resulted in the top tier being a total mess. As she had gotten a glimpse before, the bride got teary-eyed to see it this way.

Ashwini equipped patience to handle the situation by reminding herself and the bride that panic never did well. Fortunately, the cake-cutting ceremony was a little later in the schedule. It allowed Ashwini to drive home, decorate the dummy cake, and eventually replace the messy layer with the dummy layer. The bride was instructed in advance to keep the knife away from the top layer. The cake cutting ceremony and the gala event continued to pomp. And stating the obvious, the dummy layer was not a part of the feast.

While narrating the incident, she felt proud of herself and mentions the importance of wit and patience in such adversities. To her, there are no ambitions that are unachievable if planned well. Be equipped for the worst-case scenarios while not letting it bog down the spirits. She encourages other home bakers to be responsible and treat the fragile cake as an infant until the cake gets cut. She could have shrugged it off her responsibility and excused that the cake had been handed over to the client before the disaster took place. It is commendable that instead, she took care of the matter and made the bride cheery and contended as she was supposed to be.

Advice for the Upcoming Entrepreneurs

The knowledge only grows when shared. So, while talking to Ashwini, I asked for some advice to enlighten the upcoming entrepreneurs.

1. **Participate in Competitions:** She deeply emphasizes participating in competitions. If it is cumbersome or expensive to travel while carrying the cake, you may participate in the abundant

online competitions. Sharing the picture of your art while not having to step out is a boon.

2. **Engage in collaborations:** Give wings to your innovation by collaborating with other bakers. Collaborations are motivating and inspiring and an opportunity to try your hand out in different techniques. Competitions and collaborating boost us with other artists' perspectives.

3. **Track your progress**: If participating in collaborations or competitions is not your cup of tea, proliferate your progress by noting the instructions and suggestions from online media like YouTube, etc. To keep track, store pictures of the final product to compare later. After a while, you'd be surprised to realize how far you've made it.

4. **A Checklist before Launching a business**: Baking solely for self-improvement is a different game than taking up baking as a profession. Be sure to keep a tab of the vital factors like suitable registrations, appropriate packaging, fair pricing, etc. The best way out is through it, so take it at the pace that suits you. Make sure to decide on a niche and menu in accord with your expertise and interest. Note that your art reflects your enthusiasm and effort. Impulse and burdens to duplicate other bakers won't come in handy in the long run.

Some compliments from her clients and learners:

"I now have a new favorite baker! Thanks a lot Ashwini for the effort you have put in to design the cake compiling my taste and requirements. I have neither seen nor tasted a piece of cake as good as this. This cake for sure is a masterpiece in terms of taste, quality, design and appearance. The time we spent discussing the design of the cake surely paid off. It was a sheer treat to the eyes. The taste just melted away our hearts and taste buds. It was really a pleasure. Looking forward to many such occasions to come that would be graced by your work."

"I enrolled for the bean paste class to learn about the new medium, but I left with vastly more information. Not only was the course both fun and challenging but Ashwini's willingness to share all her knowledge about this new medium was invaluable. She has a calm and understandable method of teaching that truly connected and inspired me. I can't speak highly enough of this course. Thank you, Ashwini, for this session."

"It was a dream come true to take my first online workshop from a renowned cake artist. The virtual demo class almost felt real. Besides being cost effective and convenient, the workshop was highly interactive. Many thanks Ashwini for your innovative way of teaching.... looking forward to many more such opportunities in future!!"

After speaking to Ashwini, I realize that she put in prodigious work to rise in every profession she took up in her life. Starting by baking for pleasure and eventually becoming a cake artist certified as an ICES teacher is an inspiration to all women. The nine to five job sometimes makes it pain strikingly tough for women and usually mothers to take time out for their family or even themselves. Her ideology is to paint the canvas of life with the colors that the heart finds delightful. She has the vision of empowering women to take time out for themselves and not be drained and frustrated while attempting to create a healthy home environment. The home can't be healthy unless you are healthy. I wish her success and happiness to remain a tremendous inspiration for all women around.

Contact Details: +91 80081 01231

Facebook page:

https://www.facebook.com/TheDreamCakes

Instagram page:

https://www.instagram.com/thedreamcakes

Website: https://thedreamcakes.com/

Arati Mirji

First Indian Women Sugar Florist

Winner of Cake International and

Cake Masters Magazine Award

"Never undermine the power of passion. You have a very high chance of achieving anything you are passionate about." — Israelmore Ayivor

Arati Mirji is a name synonym to sugarcraft in the global cake arena. Winner of multiple contests including Cake International 2018, Cake Masters Magazine Sugar Flowers 2018, India's Top Ten Cake Artist and many others, is also a regular feature on national and international print media with the likes of Baker's Imprint, Cake Masters and FondBites. She is globally known for her special sugar crafting skills and making flowers for cake decoration which look more beautiful than the real ones.

The path to success had never been a smooth one for anyone. For most of the women the path to career building either ends after marriage or the person stops progressing further. One cannot keep blaming the circumstances all the time. We have been taught since our initial days that "Where there is a Will, there is a Way." Why not have a strong reason to pursue your dream. If you have the passion, you should strive for it and it will surely be yours. We have often experienced that many career-oriented women choose household activities as their prime task sacrificing their career and self-plans. Their life just revolves around finishing the regular household chores.

However, for Arati Mirji, age is just a number and a blockade for the mind to have a far-sighted vision. She believes that the world is rapidly changing and so is the attitude of women towards their goal. She is fond of women who go miles to pursue their passion at any stage of their life. Passion to progress, love for self-respect and willingness to fight all odds will surely make you reach a new height and establish you as a one with your own identity.

For Arati Mirji, life has always been about experimenting and learning from the outcomes. She had the habit of looking for opportunities under any form, shape, and style. With a Master's degree in psychology, Arati helped her father in his import-export business. She soon got married and became a mother to two adorable daughters. However, she had an inclination towards art which was embodied in her genes. Her love for oil painting and other art & craft forms drew her interest in creating sugar flowers, which eventually ended being her profession.

A cup of tea that changed profession and life.

Her motto and goal towards life changed in 2013 when she visited her friend's house for a cup of tea and had delicious buns there. After having those yummy homemade snacks, she got mystified that if such simple yet tasty things can be made at home, why not let it reach the masses. It was then that she decided to go further and have formal training in baking. Fortunately, Lavonne in Bangalore had started training at that time. She enrolled herself into the 6-month Diploma course of City and Guilds program.

Cooking was always her passion, but she had never tried her hands at baking until 2014.

After the completion of course, she started to bake for near and dear one's on personal reference for almost a year. Nevertheless, she wanted to achieve big.

Accidentally, she got to know about the glorious world of sugarcraft and sugar flowers. Though she started with a three-day introductory course, yet on the first day of the workshop, she knew what she was going to do henceforth. She immediately took to sugar flowers aiming to reach the epitome and got engrossed in educating herself regarding all the shades of sugar flower making through videos, tutorials, and books. Her work started getting recognition, and very soon, she started participating and winning online contests.

Sweet Symphony - Blissful Flower Harmony

Arati Mirji runs her venture in Bengaluru under the name of Sweet Symphony specializing in Sugarcraft flowers. These flowers' uniqueness took the market like a storm. They look like real flowers, but unlike natural ones, they can be stored for years together. She has treasured her flowers made five years back in glass cabinets with absorbia and silica sachets, which need to be replaced during monsoon. In many countries including the UK, these special sugar flowers are preserved as a memory momentum, the way we save our wedding photographs.

The minimum moisture males store for these sugar flowers for such a long time, a possibility. Controlled humidity by means of natural way or air conditioner or dehumidifier, can prevent these beautiful pieces from ants and bugs too.

These flowers are used to decorate magnificent celebration cakes. They have also been displayed in various International collaboration pieces where artists from all over the world get acquainted with the lifelike flowers. The idea of decorating cakes with sugar flowers is to beautify and glorify them to make special occasions memorable. The edible flowering arrangements done by sugarcraft add to the visual appeal of the cake and stay for years compared to real flowers that die within days.

Sugarcraft includes anything and everything related to cake decoration, fondant work, and structured cakes. In India, the concept of sugar flowers is a relatively new concept. The hard work of Arati Mirji has changed the scenario and bought a revolution in the baking industry.

A good teacher is always Inspiring

Arati Mirji didn't want to keep the knowledge and art limited to herself and thought of spreading it to more people. After practicing baking for a couple of years, she started conducting classes, teaching sugar flowers to individuals as well as groups in India and overseas too. Her talent was acclaimed globally and Cakeflix, the top international online cake decorating school by Paul Bradford and Sugar Geek show, another leading international online cake decorating school by Liz Marek, featured her tutorials on Sugar flowers.

Apart from a series show on Cakeflix TV, she has done many demonstrations on international Forums like Cake International, Incredible India, Cakeflix, etc. Her classes and tutorials are a source of inspiration for learning the right techniques and selecting colors while designing these pretty flowers

Only a perfect can judge others.

Once you make a name for yourself, people start looking up to you and expect more. As her art of sugarcraft bought her name and fame on the international stage, she performed her commitment as a judge with great conviction in various cake competitions too. She has been a judge in Cakeology and Fondbites.

For my fellow readers, I took the opportunity to discuss with her what matters most while judging the cakes in the competition. If you are one of those aspirants who are planning to participate in any online cake competitions or collaborations, do not miss reading the below tips from an expert herself:

1. The final product should be very appealing, eye-catching, and complimenting the theme of the competition.

2. The uniqueness and the innovation of the idea to be presented holds an essential factor.

3. The end product's feasibility with sugar flowers on a real cake is another vital point to consider.

4. The final factor includes the neatness of the endmost product. A person may have 100 ideas in her thoughts, but failure to showcase them neatly would result in non-success.

How COVID-19 pandemic impacted her business?

In March 2020, after the COVID-19 pandemic hit India and other countries worldwide, workshops and tutorials had to be halted. Earlier she was invited by various cake masters and cake collaboration organizers to take classes and present live demonstrations. Going with the trend and adapting to the latest technology, she converted her batches to online mode, which she thinks served as a boon.

These online classes helped her reach those students who were missing out on learning from her.

The new mode of imparting knowledge benefited her on the personal front, too. As being at home, she could take care and spend some time with family while pursuing her passion as well. She has a steady and reasonably large student base, most of them from being outside India. There is no stopping for the people who are keen to learn and eager to regularly attend classes to grasp the latest and right techniques & preparations in the floral category.

Even though the art of sugarcraft has been prevailing in the international arena for more than 5 decades, it is still in its nascent stage in India. It is a matter of pride for any Indian Woman to compete with artists worldwide and capture global audiences and accolades.

Advice for upcoming Women Entrepreneur

If you are committed to working towards your passion and investing your time to improvise yourself, then Sky's the limit. The people with the Best Advice are usually the ones who have been through the most. So in the same context, first-hand tips and advice from Arati Mirji, first Indian woman to win Cake Masters in the sugar flower category, is certainly a source of inspiration for the upcoming entrepreneurs.

1. Participate in Cake Collaborations: Collaborations are an excellent way to introduce and put out your work to the world who otherwise have no clue what you are doing. It's not a competition, but it's a friendly forum where each one is given a topic, and you have to make, bake and create something based on that topic. You can unveil your true artist, push yourself out of your comfort zone and compete along with the best names in the world.

Arati Mirji herself participated in Incredible India Collaboration in 2019. The event's theme was to showcase India, so she designed Ajanta and Ellora cake with sugar flowers. Though she still participates in collaboration and enjoys doing those, she is mostly involved in making arrangements for similar friendly events conducted online.

2. Think out of the box: Mrs. Mirji emphasizes increasing your involvement in different collaborations and online events so that you can expand your level of thinking and produce such a piece of art that you will be proud of. Further, she illustrates that while designing a wedding cake, the baker might have to restrict herself to the client's budget or wedding theme. In contrast, participation in collaborations opens up the door of your creativity, and you can showcase your stunning artistry based on the significant topics provided by the organizers.

3. Price your Art: While researching my book, I got an opportunity to converse with different home bakers. Many upcoming Home bakers felt that serving new recipes sometimes becomes a challenge as they have to prepare in small quantities. As the pricing increases and cannot compete with the bakery. Budget and competition limits home bakers to restrict to the same menu for a long time. As per Mrs. Mirji, it may be possible that initially, customers are hesitant to try new recipes, but your willingness and conviction can act as a catalyst in selling your product.

Nowadays, people have respect and know the value of art. She further conveys that she feels delighted that people and home bakers have gone out of their way to train and educate themselves and are successful in being able to provide customers with variety and choice in their menu. Customers have been able to find the right bakers who can bake what they want, and bakers can find the right customers who will pay money for their effort.

4. Practice well before serving the menu: Social Media has played a vital role in increasing customer's expectation and imparting knowledge to them. A vast plethora of information is available at the click of a button. Customers are bored with usual cakes and cannot be fooled by mere old products and in new variants. She advises all home bakers to practice their dishes well, educate, and upgrade oneself for in-depth knowledge of the product and ingredients. She recalls that people started appreciating her cakes and flowers from day one yet she took her own sweet time to have knowledge and expertise in sugar flowers and started taking classes after two years.

5. No end to Learning: Though she is the top sugar florist globally, she still attends tutorials to learn the latest techniques and developments required to keep herself updated. She further advises to be opportunists and upgrade oneself with the latest courses taught by the right person.

6. Patience and persistence: Designing and making Sugar flowers is not at all everyone's cup of tea. It involves patience and creativity to produce these tiny beauties. The time involved in these activities is sometimes more than the time involved in baking three basic cakes. One needs to have a lot of patience to learn the art.

Some compliments from the clients:

"The first time I learnt of Arati's expertise was when I got to see both my Engagement and Wedding cakes made by her, I was thoroughly impressed, not only were they beautiful, but they tasted divine. I believe it served as inspiration to learn the art of baking and suddenly 3 years have passed and I'm living my dream of being an artist, only cake is my canvas here! When the opportunity arose to attend Arati's SugarCraft class, I could not pass it up and signed on right away. As a teacher, her attention to detail by way of going into minute details made the 3-day classes worth it. Her passion towards her craft serves as an inspiration and I can't wait for another opportunity to gain more knowledge and insights from her."

"Each cake is a masterpiece. The flowers on her cake look so real. If you are looking for the best it has to be Arati!"

"The first time I saw Arati Ma'am work I was totally awestruck. Then to learn from her became one of my bucket lists. Finally, attend her class. It was very good. She is a beautiful person and a great teacher, and taught us all the fine details. Thank you Arati ma'am."

Contact Details: +91 9945622827

Facebook page:

https://www.facebook.com/SweetSymphonyDesserts

Instagram page: https://www.instagram.com/arati.mirji

Website : https://aratimirji.com/

Dr Asheena Batra

Dentist, Homemaker and now Home Baker

Top Ten Cake Artist in India, awarded by UK
Based Cake Masters Magazine

"Women are the largest untapped reservoir of talent in the world" - Hillary Clinton

Fatehabad is a small town in Haryana, just about in between Hisar and Sirsa. Amidst the town is a square market which comprises clinics of most kinds like ENT clinic, child specialist clinic, dental clinic, maternity homes. Out of these clinics, one dentist clinic was run by Dr Asheena Batra. Compassionate and courteous, Dr Asheena was a dentist of one of a kind. She completed her BDS in the year 2005 and practiced there for seven years.

In the year 2012, she had to move to Mohali, Punjab due to her husband's transfer. She never in her dreams thought that changing cities will change her profession too. During the time they moved to Mohali she was pregnant with her second child. The initial plan was to resume her dentistry practice after some time of delivery. Since she had free time in her hand during those days, she tried her hands-on Baking.

The first cake she baked was in 2013 for her son's Birthday which was praised by everyone around. She just fell in love with the words like Wow Wow Wow. She claims that while practicing dentistry she used to have more thankful responses. Patients did have gratitude but the appreciation that she got this time just touched her heart and gave her the motivation to bake more.

She then started baking more often, though the results were always as per the expectations - success came hand in hand with a bit of failure. It was then when she decided to go for professional training on baking and attended a four days' workshop in Chandigarh. She started practicing the recipes given by experts and started distributing cakes and desserts in neighborhood and friends.

Dr Asheena recalls that her parents were in shock when she boldly announced that it is baking that she wants to pursue as a full-time career. Like the concern of most parents, they suggested she continues her dentistry practices because she holds a professional degree in the same. Nevertheless, there was no looking back for her.

Birth of COCOMOM

One of the hardest decisions you'll ever face in life is choosing whether to walk away or try harder. The battle of qualified and experienced dentist and a newborn baker (which was not a well-known profession during those times), was continuously going in her mind for over a year. Asheena too had a tough time in deciding which path to choose.

Reminiscing those days Asheena says, "It was a really tough decision to make as I had to choose one out of passion and profession. The profession of dentistry was respectable, money earning and I already had all the required tools and setup for starting a clinic at a new place. The path of being a home baker was still faint and required a lot of new experiments and experiences. It was possible only because of the knowledge and guidance of Gurudev Sri Sri Ravi Shankar ji that helped me to take decision to make passion as my profession. The daily practice of meditation and Sudarshan Kriya helped me to face the challenges of this new profession without any major pitfall. Once I decided to go with my passion and the work which I enjoy doing, I have never regretted my decision in all these seven years."

COCOMOM was born with her courageous decision and even today the achievements during her baking journey are much more than in dentistry. Her school and college time friends have started to get in touch with her only because of her cakes. So, many old friends and acquaintances get in touch with her to congratulate her for the success that she has been able to accumulate over the years.

Win-Win Situation

Asheena started her journey single-handedly and in the initial days, she had sleepless nights due to work pressure. Now she employs a squad of eight people who come from nearby villages. They all are trained under her supervision. The work of baking, filling, frosting has been divided among the staff as per their expertise. They have been working with COCOMOM for more than four years. Though the team working hours are from nine in the morning to six in the evening, the staff is cooperative, and they too are passionate about baking and extend their working hours depending on the orders. During peak days, staff usually starts early and leaves late in the evening. Other days, they decide to stay relaxed and accept limited orders.

Asheena always believes in a win-win situation for the staff and herself. She wishes to expand her team so that she can employ many more. Her aim is to help the employment status of the country as she grows in terms of profit and productivity.

God has blessed her with a life partner who is her business partner as well. All creative designs and unique ideas of Cocomom cakes are sketched by her husband. He is not only a facilitator for COCOMOM but also takes care of all online orders along with managing Social Media handles like Facebook and Instagram for the business.

Embrace the success in the journey

As you take steps towards your baking journey, do not look upon it as hard work. Embrace the journey as the success lies here. Remember why you started and go on with your passion. And remember, even if it is small steps that you are taking, it is still moving forward. Dr Asheena was aware of this golden rule. She decided to be ambitious and practiced to gain insight with every move. With the support of her husband and family, she has established herself as the best cake artist in the tricity of Chandigarh, Mohali and Panchkula. Not only she specializes in designer cakes but also has the expertise and caters to everything related to dessert tables like cupcakes, macrons, push pops, cake seekers, mini desserts, donuts, and so on.

Her vacations are also planned according to her business schedule. Since she has a team to manage, she takes one or two short breaks in the year and schedule trips to those places where she can purchase bakery related stuff and other things. She giggles while confessing that on special occasions like birthdays and anniversaries, she solely demands new tools and instruments that can be used in her bakery instead of any other materialistic gift.

She has never been worried about the competition as she is very confident and comes up with creative ideas for cakes. This was not an overnight achievement; it took resilience for gaining such abilities. Entrepreneurial skills also helped her achieve this.

As a home baker, she many times has to suggest what design will actually look great for their occasions as many times people will have no idea what to order, so she has to give input and suggestions which are mutually agreed by both. For instance, once a lady demanded the face replica cake for the first birthday of her son, and so she suggested better that she go for a cute cake instead. There are times when customers ask for a non-seasonal flavor and hence, it is upon her to advise them into better options. Oftentimes she and the staff have to freeze and store seasonal ingredients so that they can be used for a longer time.

A positive way forward

As an entrepreneur, if you think everything will work out as hunky-dory and as predicted, then you are not doing a good job. Experience comes from bad experiences and they enlighten you. Asheena too had faced those disgraceful moments but what she has not forgotten is the lesson she learned from those moments.

One of the catastrophes faced by her was when a customer received a tilted three-tier cake delivered via Uber. Instead of getting disheartened, she chose to turn the shortcomings into lessons. She understood that delegating the responsibility of delivering delicate cakes through such mediums is futile. She decided to take the responsibility of delivering such cakes herself and considering sending small cakes through cabs.

Another instance where she felt helpless was when she was taking a gigantic eight-tier whipped cream cake to deliver to a customer and an unnoticed speed breaker caused a jerk and the cake slid inside the dickey. As a result, the third tier from bottom got smashed. Smart as she is, always carries extra cream and tools to do the final touch up of the cake and it acted as a savior. She did not let her efforts go in vain. The take from this is sometimes things do not go as predicted and you feel discouraged but do not let anything or anyone come in the way of your baking success. Do hope for the best and yet, be prepared for the worst.

Advice for upcoming Women Entrepreneurs in the Baking Industry:

It is said that 'Give neither advice nor salt, until you are asked for', so we asked Asheena for some advice for upcoming Women Entrepreneurs in the baking industry. If you wish to be successful like her, stick with these guidelines she has drawn.

1. Have patience with all things: She advises to be very patient and always start from the basics. Commencing phase of every business is always the learning phase, grab as much knowledge as you can. Just don't try to fetch any order that involves complicated designs and more money until you are confident and experienced. Stepping up slowly is the key to success.

2. Start with a basic Setup: Her advice to women who are starting their journey as Home Bakers are to start small. Be it a hobby or business all that is required is an oven and some basic tools. But as you grow as a baker do not hesitate to invest in different moulds, tools and most importantly, new techniques.

3. Prepare a menu list well in advance: Her suggestion to upcoming bakers is to have a list of selected flavors prepared in accord to whatever they can offer and is feasible. This tip will definitely reduce chaos and help in the smooth functioning of your business.

4. Show your digital presence: She believes that it is an important step for home bakers to portray their presence to the world. Always be presentable and active on social media viz Facebook and Instagram. This would not only be a portfolio but also will help in getting orders. Her previous work on Social media grabbed her the following awards:

Achievements till date:

- Winner of Indian Cake Awards in Sculpted cake category - 2019

- Top 10 cake artist in Cake masters UK magazine - 2019

- Biggest cake designed by her was of 400 kg. It was made in 9 days at The Art Of Living International Center at Bangalore, for the 62nd birthday of Gurudev Sri Sri Ravi Shankar.

- Her work and tutorials have been featured multiple times in magazines like FondBites and CakeMasters.

- She is a jury member for the Global Master Cake Competition.

How COVID-19 pandemic impacted her business?

On March 24, 2020, India's Prime Minister Mr Narender Modi announced a nationwide lockdown due to the COVID-19 pandemic. Everyone was forced to stay at home and people started craving for different bakery items. Home bakers turned out to be rescuers in this situation. Asheena was able to continue taking orders for simple cakes and not designer ones as her staff was not available. She states that before the pandemic they used to cater for bigger events like weddings. But, during the pandemic, weddings were either not taking place or were not such a gala occasion so her whole focus and effort were in small cakes. Furthermore, to avoid the risk of contamination, delivery of cakes was also done by her.

Compliments from Clients:

"Found on Instagram while searching for a good cake bakery in Chandigarh, Mohali.

The way of accepting orders, asking for each and every detail and providing suggestions was wonderful.

Such a delicious Unicorn themed cake and donuts for my little 1st birthday girl.

Color matching with the dress was fantabulous!! Thank You so much for your beautiful creation.

Overall was a great experience, hoping for many more cakes from cocomom in future!!"

"I highly recommend, if someone really wants a good-looking delicious cake, Cocomom is the place. I have become a great fan of their cakes. I have ordered numerous cakes and every-time it's a WOW... Thumbs up "

"Dr Asheena is the best cake artist I've come across my whole life. I can't thank her enough for all she did for me! Thank you so so so much ma'am! She has magic in her hands, does wonders She creates a wonderful masterpiece in such a short notice for me. Cooperated so much. I wish she could deliver her wonderful cakes here in Delhi as well. Highly highly recommended I would surely recommend everyone to reach Cocomom cakes for the best piece of art!"

You can always have a virtual tour of the real creativity and talent of Dr Asheena Batra on her social pages. I am sure once you browse through her Facebook or Instagram page, in first place you would be amazed and forced to think if it is a real cake. She has been able to conceptualize thousands of cake designs for hundreds of customers, resulting in satisfied and happy clientele. Her miraculous cakes will drool you out and would rather leave you in a confused state in deciding which are her best cakes. Be it a wedding cake or a figure replica cake, from the design to color combinations, every minute details are worth observing. If you are living or travelling in or around the beautiful city of Chandigarh, make sure that you order one of the best designer cakes from this talented cake artist. All my heartfelt wishes for the lady beautiful to accomplish her dreams!

Contact Details: +91 9781644740

Facebook page:

https://www.facebook.com/cocomom.cakes

Instagram page:

https://www.instagram.com/cocomom.cakes

Bani Nanda

Pastry Queen of India

Founder of Miam Pâtisserie,

Entrepreneur at age of 25

"Build your business success around something that you love — something that is inherently and endlessly interesting to you." —Martha Stewart

Motivation is a hoax. Yes, you heard it right. There are trillions of motivation theories and videos on the internet but leadership is one skill that cannot be generated by a mere motivating quote. It is way complex but extremely simple and feasible at the same time. Gone are those days when say, leaders are born and not made. You can be a leader and an entrepreneur at any age, regardless of your gender, skill, education, or age. The story of the Pastry Queen is one story to look for annihilating the complexity and taboos.

MIAM means yummy in French. Miam Patisserie was founded in June 2015 by Bani Nanda who was just 25 years old when she started her journey. The reason why she chose a French name for her business unit was the fact that she was and is still impressed by France and owes a lot to France. Graduated in Physics from Gargi College in Delhi University, she chose a career in the sphere of pastries and desserts. Before beginning her pastry shop in South Delhi, she had graduated from Le Cordon Bleu in Paris and then worked as a pastry chef in Dalloyau and The Oberoi.

Filmmaker Mira Nair, cricketer Suresh Raina, rapper Honey Singh, politician Shehzad Poonawala, and former cricketer Kapil Dev and many other famed people love to shop from Miam. The range of customized cakes and desserts for all moods has won several, forever happy customers. It was opened with the motive to bring a bit of Paris to Delhi and to introduce people to the French flavor in pastry as those were not so popular in India.

As per Vivian Greene, "Life is not about waiting for the storm to pass, It's about learning how to dance in the rain". Bani quit her job at the Oberoi Hotel in January 2015 because of a shoulder injury as It was quite severe. She had to stay at home for a considerable amount of time which she utilized to conceive, plan and conceptualize her business at her parents' home in SDA, Delhi.

She had always been inspired by food! She had grown up watching cooking shows on TV and her mother, Charu Nanda, who has been running a home bakery since 2011. Baking had always been an inseparable part of her life as they never ordered birthday cakes from outside.

The Secret of getting ahead in getting started

Bani was continuing her graduation in Physics and exploring different opportunities in the related field but all doors lead to proceeding with a master's degree in physics. During the summer break in her college days, she took up a two-week internship at The Leela Palace, Chanakyapuri. She was so much inspired and propelled by The head chef - Chef Alam, that by the seventh day, she had decided to take her career as a pastry chef.

Her decision was a surprise for her parents too, but still, they supported her in all her decisions. Under her parents' guidance and support, she completed the nine-month Diplôme de Pâtisserie course at Le Cordon Bleu in Paris.

Paris Memories

She not only learned the art of pastry making from Paris but travelled and explored Paris and Western Europe during that time. The prime motive of the budgeted trips was to visit cafés, bakeries and restaurants to learn the functionality and business model.

In her interview with us, she affirms that her visit to a couple of chocolate shops in Belgium inspired her to design the layout of her store and display counters artistically. This is the secret behind her aesthetic sense. Her exposure leads to the birth of Miam.

After completing her degree, she worked for almost a year at Dalloyau - which is a 400-year-old pastry shop in Paris. Her experience helped her to learn and grasp the management and organizational skills. Dalloyau has multiple stores in Paris. The pastries and other products here were supplied from the main kitchen which was outside Paris. Since she got an opportunity to work with one of the biggest suppliers of pastries, she grasped the art of precision and quality maintenance during bulk orders.

She reinvented the pastry market in Delhi. People indulged only in American pastry and had no idea about neoclassical French pastry.

Together Everyone Accomplishes More (TEAM)

As per Bani, her family is the founder team for her. She recollects how her family supported and helped her to start her home bakery. Her grandmother's room was converted to a kitchen. She is still operating her business from here. Her father helped her to get the required equipment for baking. Since her mother is a home baker, she too had contacts and sources to buy the printed boxes to sell her products. Her sister designed the brand logo for her. So, setting up the kitchen was a family project.

At present, she is a well-established entrepreneur with a team of 8 members. Initially she had only herself and her assistant but now her team has 3 chefs and 2 managers. She addresses her team as her backbone as she firmly believes if the team is not strong, it is tough to accomplish your dream.

Her husband, Akshay Handa, is not only her life partner but business partner too. He has been the business head of MIAM and taking care of logistics and operations since 2018. His experience in operations has helped MIAM to grow, expand and set up its flagship studio and café.

Specialization

Morihei Ueshiba, famous Japanese Martial Artist and founder of the Martial Art of Aikido said, "Even the most powerful human being has a limited sphere of strength. Draw him outside of that sphere and into your own, and his strength will dissipate." Bani Nanda follows this philosophy with full confidence. She claims that innovation and the courage to be different from others are the secrets behind her success.

MIAM is well known for French pastries, cakes, and macarons in the Delhi region. Like every business has some signature products, so do MIAM. The most talked and ordered products of MIAM include Passion Fruit and Milk Chocolate Macarons and Dark chocolate and salted caramel entremet. Entremet is a layered French dessert that was introduced to the people of Delhi by Bani Nanda. She also offers chocolate mousses in a 3D shaped layered cake.

Bani claims that in MIAM flavor of the dish is always given utmost importance. She always emphasizes preparing dishes from natural and seasonal ingredients instead of additives or preservatives. If you have ever visited or ordered from her, you would become a die-hard fan of her presentation skills also.

Nothing worth having comes easy

Roy T.Bennett has mentioned in his inspirational book The Light in the Heart, "Life is about accepting the challenges along the way, choosing to keep moving forward, and savoring the journey." For Ms. Nanda, establishing and continuing this entrepreneurship was never so easy. She had to push herself through casual sexism. Dealing with vendors was the biggest challenge that she faced as they didn't seem to think businesswomen could experience any kind of success.

Facing such challenges and rising the ladder of success needs courage and confidence. The motive of this book is to inspire my readers and to bring light to the fact that success comes only to those who overcome the challenges with courage and positivity.

We wished to know how she is handling competition in this competitive world to which she replied, "I am not a competitive person and I'm not aggressive with business. I am very passionate and confident. That's my way forward! There were many bad experiences which have made me strong and constantly rethink Miam."

With her dedication and strong will power to succeed, she could constantly streamline the process. She focused on good packaging and capped that with setting systems in places. This has led to evolving herself as a successful home baker. Along with running a Pâtisserie, she also conducts many workshops for aspiring pastry chefs and home bakers. She has always focused on her unique style and believes in no set menu system.

Advice to for upcoming Home Bakers:

Bani Nanda is a very practical person who has achieved success at a very young age. Apart from baking, she loves travelling. She remarks that her trip is a source of knowledge, and to grasp whatever she can from that place - be it the preparation or presentation style.

She believes that home bakers are churning out some lovely stuff and this is helping in empowering many women. The only piece of advice which she wanted to shred is to develop a unique style in your venture. She believes many home bakers try to copy other bakers which is not a healthy way to proceed. Your creativity and uniqueness will take you further and far. So always isolate yourself from the masses with her inventiveness and imagination.

She is a firm believer in the fact that everyone is the perfect version of themselves and if you give yourself the proper time you will soon be able to explore your creativity which will make you different from others.

Compliments from Clients:

"Bani you make 'Heaven-on-earth' type of desserts. Everything is on-point. Yummiest Macarons and Red Velvet Macaron cake i've ever had! 🩶 *"*

"I ordered an assortment of macrons, and they were delicious. Loved the dark chocolate and red velvet ones. The packaging is really pretty, and the box of macrons made a wonderful gift!"

"Bani you are pure genius. Loved loved loved the dark chocolate and salted caramel cake. Can't wait to try out the others. ☺ *"*

Contact Details: +91 9871441164

Facebook page:

https://www.facebook.com/miampatisserie

Instagram page:

https://www.instagram.com/miampatisserie

Website: https://www.miampatisserie.com/

Aashu Shah

Ex-Entrepreneur in Fashion Industry,

Homemaker, Home Baker and Cake Artist.

Introduction

Aashu Shah, an amazing Cake Artist and a mother of a 14-year-old daughter hails from the royal city of Hyderabad. Entrepreneurship is not new to her as she was already settled as a successful entrepreneur in the Fashion Industry. Being creative since childhood, her love to decorate things propelled her into Fashion designing. She was running a tailoring Unit for Women from 2002-2006. Her business unit undertook orders for designing and supplying uniforms for Hotels, Food Chains, Retail chains etc.

Like many other new moms, she had to take a forced break in her business after her daughter's birth. The break got little extended as the family shifted to Bangalore in January 2007 and then to Kolkata in April 2011. Once her daughter grew and started becoming independent, the thought of getting back to action occurred to her. It is then, her love for baking started, and she seized another opportunity to use her creativity and passion for adornment.

Cakes A'Fair - An affair with cakes

As rightly said, "There is no glory in practice, but without practice there is no glory". In the famous movie 'Karate Kid' released in 1984, the coach too emphasized on practicing the basics which resulted in expertise movements. Aashu

Shah began her experiments with baking in the year 2015. In her interview she stated that she used to bake and decorate about six to eight cakes in one day, just for practice. Phewww!!! What a dedication to learn and reach the height of perfection.

Her first cake which turned out good enough to be a professional one was a fondant cake, which she made for her daughter's birthday party in the same year. It was a hit among the guests and that is where her journey began as a home baker and orders started pouring in. It was the start of a journey with cakes which the world now knows as **Cakes A'Fair...!!!**

Cakes A'fair also symbolizes 'An affair with cakes. The way she is passionate and creative about baking cakes, it is no less than having an affair. Baking and Cake Art gave her an insight to be able to showcase her creative imagination and allowed her to communicate with her inner perception. As she moved on this became her passion and eventually passion turned into profession.

Achievements till date

While I interviewed Best Cake Artists and Home Bakers for my book, to mine and everyone's surprise these artists come from different backgrounds. Hardly few bakers got these skills inherited. Most of them have found their own way by hit and trial, overcoming all challenges, setting up their own goals, targets and achievements are no less than benchmarks for many amateur bakers.

Before I highlight the challenges and the journey of this Home baker, I would like to highlight her achievements and awards till date.

- ✓ She was a Finalist representing India in the Occasional Cakes Category of the Im Cake Star International Online Cake Competition 2020 hosted by By Bora Sugar Paste Company.
- ✓ Recognized as India's Top 50 and Hyderabad's Top 25 Home Bakers in 2019 and promoted to India's Top 25 and Hyderabad's Top 10 Home Bakers in 2020 by a website on Home Bakers.
- ✓ Participation in the INDIAN CULTURE online Competition in the Sculpture Cake Category where she had created a replica of "THE CHARMINAR", the famous monument in Hyderabad. This gave her an identity and space among some of the best artists in the industry.
- ✓ Participation in the Bangladeshi Culture, Art and Heritage online cake competition in the Bust Cake Category where she created a Bust Cake of the famous Bangladeshi political figure - "Moulana Hameed Khan Bhasani". This was her first bust cake which earned her appreciation from masses.
- ✓ Participated in "Art of Pottery – An International Cake Art Collaboration", where she created a Modelling Chocolate Bust figure, 'A Veiled Lady'. This collaboration got her work featured in some of the best National & International Cake Magazines like American Cake Decorating Magazine, Cake Masters Magazine and Cake Decoration &

Sugarcraft Magazine from the UK and Fondbites Magazine from India.

✓ Cake tutorial of her designer cake "Robe Geniale" was featured in the India edition of the CAKE MASTERS MAGAZINE.

✓ Participated in the LIBYAN "CAKE COLLABORATION" where she created Modeling Chocolate Hand with Henna design having Arabic scripture conveying Eid wishes.

Success is a Journey not a Destination

As the name Home bakers infer, most of the women start their journey from home as one-woman army. From baking to designing, marketing to delivery, everything has to be handled by them initially. Aashu's journey also is no different but what I admire her for is her vision in different matters. So, I take this as an opportunity and present my conversation with this wonder woman directly to my readers.

Me: What are the challenges you faced during your journey?

"For any home baker the biggest challenge is to market and price their product. When compared with the market, products by home bakers are seen as expensive but the amount of effort which goes into customizing the cakes and high-quality ingredients used are seldom noticed. However, there is also a segment which now supports home bakers and that is what keeps me going."

Me: How is your business streamlined in terms of baking, packaging and delivering so many orders?

"Streamlining happens with time and experience. I was able to streamline my baking and packaging with help of some of the best-in-class products, ingredients, tools and equipment and by adding the experience gained over a period of time. Managing deliveries was initially a challenge as I used to deliver the cakes myself or my husband used to do it on my behalf, and we still do it within manageable distances, this gives me an opportunity to build the 'Customer Connect'. A few clients pick up the order themselves and for others, we use Uber, Ola and other delivery services available to deliver the cakes."

Me: How are you handling competition as so many bakers coming up?

"Competition is good for this creative business of Baking. It inspires me and gives me a chance to be at my best day after day. I believe in giving my clients what they want in my cakes, best design/customization and the best taste. This keeps bringing them back to Cakes A'Fair for more."

Me: How do you handle failure?

"Every failure is a challenge and an opportunity. Among the initial ones I had faced, the truly testing ones were getting the consistency in weight, texture, sharp edges and other detailing right. But with time and practice, and with the help of expert advice, I learned the art of consistency and what was once difficult, started becoming easy and now I teach the same to buddy Home Bakers through my workshops and demonstrations."

Me: Do you want your daughter to follow your footsteps?
"My daughter, Noopur, is also passionate about Baking and started baking at the age of 9. She bakes cakes, Brownies, Doughnuts, Cheese Cakes Cookies, Breads, Pizza Bases and more. She bakes for orders by her clients and her Brownies and Cheese Cakes are their top selling favorites. She has already delivered Live Demo classes on Facebook and Instagram on Baking Walnut Choco-Chip. Her recipes were also posted by a website on Home Bakers.

Don't be the same, be BETTER

Aashu started as a self-trained Baker and Cake Artist and as her interest in this field grew stronger, she further decided to enhance her skills and learn more from some of the best professionals. Hence, she attended a few workshops from experts of Baking industry.

- Wedding Cakes workshop by Rumana Jaseel

- Royal Icing Cookies Workshop by Marta Torres

- Face Anatomy Workshop by Samie Ramchandran

These training sessions helped her to intensify the skills and artistry of baking and decorating. Though she has mastery in all types of cakes, most of her orders happen to be theme-based and designer ones such as Wedding Cakes and other Occasional Cakes. One of the milestone cakes designed by her is a replica of "THE CHARMINAR", a famous monument in Hyderabad.

Baking is her ultimate passion and hence she keeps learning new things and always takes up challenging work.

Sharing it, is the first step to humanity".

"Gaining Knowledge, is the first step to wisdom.

Apart from increasing her skill set, she also believes in sharing her information with her fellow bakers. She has demonstrated multiple times live on social media her skills of Glazed cakes, Edible Lace and Peony Flowers. Moreover, she is also specialized in conducting online workshops on Basic, Fondant, Wedding, Structured and Hanging Cakes.

Collaborations are a great platform to display your real talent. Mrs. Shah has also participated in different Global collaborations sharing stages with global bakers and cakes artists. She had been very successful in presenting herself in collaborations like FAB Recipe Collaboration, Libyan Cake Collaboration and Art of Pottery - An international cake art collaboration and many more.

Advice for upcoming Women Entrepreneurs in Baking:

For a country as big as India, there is enough and more space and market for Home Bakers. The future looks really bright for those who want to do and achieve something for the community they are in. This also means that the consumers will have more choice and variety delivered by someone in their neighborhood.

It would be unfair if we do not get a piece of advice from a woman who has set standards in the Baking industry with her hard work and dedication. I am sure by following her advice and footsteps, you too can reach the level where she is.

Never stop learning: Baking is like an ocean. New techniques and innovations crop up every day, so keep learning.

Deliver the best: Never compromise on the quality of your ingredients, as it is the quality and taste which bring customers back to you.

Never give up: This is a demanding journey and you will face your set of failures. Be prepared to put in hard work as it will always translate into success.

Compliments from Clients:

"Amazing at flavor 😋. most importantly its so soft n moist also it is exactly as per the picture of the cake that you want it to be 🙂. I love her work and wild always recommend her cakes 😊."

"Awesome creativity and extremely Talented. Must Must Must. Try the all mix fresh fruits...its heavenly. The quality and the price is the Best in the market......"

"Wonderful collection of cakes and desserts. Perfectly done for any occasions asked for. Awesome taste, excellent service & no words to describe the taste.... Yummy, mouth watering... Loving it "

Contact Details: +919231242432, +918017642124

Facebook page: https://www.facebook.com/Cakes.A.Fair

Instagram page: https://www.instagram.com/cakes.a.fair

Nitisha Jain

Homemaker and cake artist

Winner of Great American Cake

and Wedding competition

"Follow your passion — and if you don't know what it is, realize that one reason for your existence on earth is to find it." —Oprah Winfrey

'CrEatables' - The dictionary meaning of CrEatables is "That can be created". Thinking on similar lines Nitisha Jain, initially a home maker, created and owned her business as **'CrEatables'** which she refers to as Creative Eatables. The name best suits her creativity. The uniqueness about her work is the customization of creativity which ignites excitement in her effort. Interesting thing about her cakes is that they are eggless and all her customers are egg eating.

Nitisha was born, brought up and got married in the city of Chennai. In 2012, she moved to the US with her husband and a two-year-old son. She started with home baking which was then transformed to catering orders in the US in the same year. She is now a mother of two sons 10 and 4 years, and lives in a joint family in Chennai. There are other home bakers in the family too who help Nitisha when she has big orders or any milestone cakes to bake.

She gives all credit of the success to her loving husband who motivated and helped her in improving in all aspects in her venture. Be it the ingredients or pricing of the cake, calculation of profits or dealing with clients, he was always beside her to make virtuous decisions. Nitisha is always thankful to him from the bottom of her heart as she says she had skills and her husband polished her.

As rightly said, necessity pushes you to uncover your potential. This baker too unfolded her potential of baking in order to heal her craving for cake. Her story is inspirational as well as motivating just like a baby taking his first step to walk. I always believe if a baby does not take those steps, he or she can never walk in life. Similarly, if Nitisha had not dared to bake her first cake, she would not have reached the level where she is today.

"Sometimes bad things have to happen before good things can." — Becca Fitzpatrick, Crescendo

June 2012: US

A casual Sunday, she planned her day to visit Christiana Mall in Delaware with her husband and 2-year-old son. After a tiring visit and shopping, they went to the food court to have their lunch. The food court had a special section for cakes. There were beautiful and colorful cakes, presented artistically in glass showcases. People were standing in queues to place their order. Those who were getting cake pieces had an expression of victory on their faces. Nitisha also got so fascinated towards them. However, she couldn't grab a single piece for herself as all cakes had egg in it, and she being from a Jain family, preferred pure vegetarian. The craving to have cake lasted in her mind for days of seeing it. Even after trying a number of other places in the hope to get at least some basic eggless cake, but to her disappointment she couldn't get anywhere.

THIS was the time when she took the matter seriously and planned to bake her first cake. And then started the series of baking cakes. With her obsession for getting perfect cake, she started baking every three or four days and the consumers of her cake were only she and her husband. Like any wise man, her husband could also eat only a few times. The reason was not the taste but too much of the dish in a week loses interest. On one hand, her husband was the real critic and helped her improve the taste, the softness, the texture of the cakes, however at times he would get annoyed too as to how much cake he can eat.

To improvise her baking skills, she then started distributing in Jain temples in Delaware. The first order of 500 cupcakes was ordered by the President of the same temple.

Angel Customers

By word of mouth, she slowly started getting more orders. She recalls that during those years getting cake orders was not an easy task. The order frequency was once in 7-10 days. As rightly said, slow and steady wins the race. In no time she got some "Angel customers". The term Angel customers is used by Nitisha as she explains, "The customers who really hold your hand and help you to climb the ladder of success". And believe me, every business has some angel customers. So trust your instincts and grab every opportunity to get those 'Angel Customers'. Your journey may be long but with those angels along with you, you will never feel alone.

Till this time she had been working only with butter cream and whipped cream. There was a fear inside her of using the fondant. After one year once she started to work with fondant, got so attracted. In her own words she says, "Fondant was like playing with clay. Figurine work was so nice. I just loved modelling small-small things - shoes, shopping bags, etc. Fondant helped me in taking my cakes to the next level as I always had fascination about art and craft, so I could use Fondant to beautify my cakes with whatever design I want. Many times icing will be whipped cream or butter cream but topping will be fondant. I was just in love with a fondant".

She then attended various modelling workshops to enhance her skills. She mastered the art of creating dolls and figures which look so real. All figures have clear body parts like chin, lips, etc. which make them resemble more to humans than dolls.

Participating and winning at Great American Cake and Wedding competition, US - October 2015

Soon after she got confidence in baking and a satisfying response from her customers, she got an opportunity to participate in the 'Great American Cake and Wedding competition'. The theme of the competition was 'Autumn' and Nitisha had no idea what to design for competition. Many questions kept arising in her mind related to baking, design, color of the cake. She even did not know what parameters would be considered, so kept pinging the organizers to guide her as it was the first time for her. She recalls that organizers were very supportive and helping and tried their best to guide her. For more than a week, her nights were sleepless, just to plan and design the cake for upcoming competition.

Since her birth roots are Indian, she added Indian design to the cake. A 4-tier cake showcasing a Royal Indian wedding - Bride and Groom figures on the top tier and eight women figures on the wall of the second tier. Tier first and third had all over designs of different things depicting Indian weddings - from palki to shehnai, elephants and horses - all was carved on the cake.

The venue was almost three hours' drive from her residence and as per rules, all participants had to assemble in the venue by 8am. With the intention to reach the destination well in time, they started from their home at around 4am in chilling October. Handling cake in their own vehicle was no less than handling the baby. On reaching the venue, started the work of assembling the cake as per her design. The masterpiece after assembling looked just fantastic and eye-catcher. Judges were just startled about the fantabulous presentation and how she designed all this in just less than ten days.

Competing with cake artists from different parts of the US and world was a milestone in itself. The event was a learning experience for life long. She had never witnessed such magnificent cake designs earlier. Anxiety and nervousness prevailed in her throughout the event. The results were announced by the end of day.

Wow!! She won the 3rd prize in that category and made everyone felt proud of her. It boosted Nitisha's morale and her confidence to next level.

In the coming year she again participated in different categories - like cupcakes, celebration cakes and won prizes in all categories. Then there was no looking back for her thereafter. Her crazy fan customers in the US would travel miles to get cake from her.

Fall of a cake

Every success comes with failures and bad experiences. Those moments are the best moments as they teach us lessons. So always take these moments as opportunities to learn and excel more in the field you are pursuing.

Nitisha got an order of fruit cake from Anita, a good friend of hers. It was not the first time when she was baking and delivering such a cake. Though she had mastered the art of baking, yet always tried to add some variation to the cake. Her adamant nature of not repeating the design on the cake provoked her to look for ways to make it different from previous baked cakes.

This time she baked a beautiful Heart shaped fruit cake. The icing was done neatly with white buttercream, with a lot of fruit filling. Small pieces of fresh fruit - apples, mangoes, strawberries, grapes were adding to the beauty and were making the cake look so colorful. The unique feature of the cake was that apart from fresh fruits, the cake had 3 figurines(dolls) on it. Skewers were used to make figurine stands on cake. Nitisha was very excited and proud of her creativity. She clicked a few pics from different angles to post on her social media pages. While she was on her thoughts about the title and description of the cake, Anita came to collect the cake. She got excited to see the cake and hugged and thanked Nitisha so many times. Soon she carried the cake from the dining table with utmost care and started walking towards the main gate. She had hardly taken seven eight steps and had not reached the main gate, when Nitisha heard Anita scream. Nitisha was startled, meanwhile Anita turned and with a low voice said, "Looks like cake has Cracked".

"What!!" asked Nitisha. The moment for both was as if it's not the cake but the floor cracked.

Nitisha came running and took the cake back to the dining table carefully to check what happened. Since the cake had a lot of fruit and weight of skewers, it had become too moist and the cake sank and fell on itself. She tried to fix whatever was possible at that time and had to compensate her friend with another complimentary cake later.

Nitisha remembers this as the most heartbreaking and embarrassing moment in her life. But as rightly said mistakes are the best 'gurus' and a successful person always learns from his or her mistakes. Nitisha always takes care not to repeat her mistakes, but take a lesson and move on.

How COVID-19 pandemic affected her business?

She is known for baking and delivering very tall cakes. Since March 24, 2020, after the Prime Minister of India, Mr Narendra Modi announced nationwide lockdown, weddings and other celebrations have paused for some time and then reduced, so she did not take any orders. Some loyal customers approached her for simple cakes during this time but since she considers herself a cake artist and not an average baker, she doesn't take orders for simple cakes. She has always looked for orders where she can show her artistic skills, play adventurous and try new things.

She has used this time to spend with her family, especially kids as she holds the opinion that as a home baker, she missed a lot of time, spending with family.

After almost seven months Nitisha resumed her business with the same zeal and passion. I am sure her loyal clients will be eagerly waiting for the cakes baked by her and her business will flourish even better after this break.

Advice for upcoming Women Entrepreneurs:

This is the advice from the Homemaker who has established herself well as Home Baker. Nitisha insists every upcoming Women Entrepreneur to just follow the passion, be it any profession. If you have any spark within you, just go and make fire out of it. Don't lose the spark that makes you - YOU.

Home Baking is easy business to start as it does not need a fancy setup to start. If you are talented and passionate, but have financial constraints, starting something from home is always a good option. Just give you 100% and you can go through a long way.

Achievements and Milestone cakes:

1. In the US, her last cake was based on a jungle theme that was mind-blowing. It had 3 tiers and all were stacked on each other on edible bark.

2. In 2019, during New Year she designed the Royal Prince and Royal Princess theme cake which were miraculous cakes with its minute details.

3. In November 2019, she got an order for 1500 sugar decorated custom cookies for the wedding.

Compliments from Clients:

"I ordered a birthday cake and cookies with CrEatables. Nitisha was extremely professional and proactive. She gave me suggestions and was also very open to taking mine. She understood my requirement very well and worked around it. The cake and cookies turned out very well. With Nitisha, while the output was also very good, the highlight for me was the smoothness with which she handled the entire process which made it a pleasure to work with her."

"Awesome work Nitisha. Rio theme cake was extraordinary. OMG those birds in the cake look so real and very appealing. Your cake was the showstopper and my Guest was super happy with the taste. Next comes the cup cake, I was wondering, how much perfection u r giving to the things you do. Kudos to you dear. Waiting to order more from you"

Wow, Nitisha is absolutely amazing! I called her only 2 days before the party and asked her if she could do something for me. She not only understood my budget limitations, but made a cake that received compliments from EACH guest at the party! She is very detail oriented, super creative, talented, professional and punctual. She made the cake beautiful and yummy. The cake looked and tasted very delicious with the flavors of butterscotch crunch and piña colada. Everyone raved about cake at the party. Thank You Nitisha!

I feel Nitisha is a true professional, and has wonderful skill in creating cakes. The way she has paved her path in the baking industry is truly an inspiration for all who are exploring their talents. If you are ready to put in so much effort and dedication in whatever you are doing or planning to do, then place and time is no hindrance in your success. Her creativity is nothing less than a virtual treat for eyes. And if you are in Chennai or nearby do make your special occasions more memorable with cakes from a great cake artist!!

Contact Details: +91 3027657574, +91 6379485114

Facebook page: https://www.facebook.com/egglesscreatables

Instagram page: https://www.instagram.com/creatables

Megha Kwatra Madan

Dental Surgeon at Fortis and now a Cake artist

Top Ten Cake Artist in India

'When a woman rises up in glory, her energy is magnetic and her sense of possibility contagious." - Marianne Williamson

If you ask any Engineer or doctor today, what profession would you like to choose in the future, the immediate answer that you can expect is "Have you gone insane?". Why would a doctor, a surgeon or an engineer change his profession when we know these professions offer dream come true opportunities and jobs that are highly paying. The success story of this home baker will inspire you too as she did not plan to change her profession when she took a break from her nine to five job in a reputed hospital.

Megha Kwatra Madan, a dental surgeon by choice, holds a professional degree in Bachelor of Dental Surgery (BDS) from Subharti Dental College, Meerut and an international diploma in cosmetic dentistry from NYU College of dentistry, New York. She had worked for five years in both public and private hospitals including the esteemed Fortis Hospital, New Delhi. Satisfied and contented with her professional job she never in her wildest dreams thought of quitting dentistry any day.

Fate is what you have given, but destiny is what you make out of it. Eight years ago, when her daughter was just forty days old, she got epileptic attack with froth coming from her mouth, eyes dilated and mouth twisted. She was rushed to hospital to find a cyst in her brain during an MRI scan. Since she was getting frequent seizures, her doctor recommended refraining from activities like swimming, driving, dentistry, etc. for a while. During that one year, while she was home bound, she thought of utilizing her time by learning something new. Since tender age she had an inclination towards cooking and kept trying new recipes but baking was one thing that she was lagging. She recollects the first cake baked by her in her life was at the age of 30.

Passion to Profession

Mrs. Megha is a very popular name in Delhi and NCR when designer cakes are referred. She is the founder and runs her cake studio under the name of Studio Cake O' Luv in Noida. In her interview with us, she shared that she started baking with the sole intention of being able to make cakes every year for her daughter's birthday. While she was learning and practicing baking, she realized cake decoration and fondant art are her area of interests, so she tried to dig deep into it by experimenting new designs frequently and started sharing it on her social media. That's when she got noticed by her friends and family who further pushed her in taking orders for them. With a smile on her face, she admits that she did not even realize when her hobby and passion turned into a professional career.

Where there's a whisk, there's a way!!

There is a famous quote by Sukant Ratnakar, "We do not need to attend classroom training programs for everything. Observation opens the windows of knowledge around us." On the same line though Mrs. Megha Kwatra also does not hold any professional degree from any of the institutes in the baking industry, but she considers herself fortunate enough to have attended multiple workshops and tutorials by some of the best cake artists in India and abroad. She considers herself majorly self-taught who kept on experimenting with new designs and techniques and her mistakes became the biggest teacher during her journey.

Today, she specializes in designer fondant cakes that range from cute birthday cakes, anti-gravity structured cakes, elaborate multi-tiered wedding cakes, chandelier cakes and entremets. Recently she has developed a love for sugar flowers, and have incorporated them in a lot of her cakes. With her experience she has realized which cake art form and techniques she is more comfortable with, so she accepts orders accordingly.

She considers being a process oriented and an organized home baker is her strength to reach to a level where she is today. Since she has been into this profession from the last six years and has worked really hard, over a period of time she has drawn a lot of learnings from her experience. She does everything on her own, takes limited orders that she is comfortable with but makes sure to delight her clients with her design and creativity.

Little Steps, Big Achievements

She has been recognized as one of India's Top 25 home bakers in the year 2019 and then promoted to India's Top 10 home baker for 2020 by a website on home bakers. She has been credited as one of Delhi's Top 10 home bakers for consecutive years 2019 and 2020 by the same organizers.

She along with her team (Tough Cookies) had won India's first ever live cake war competition held in Mumbai by Cakeology in 2019

Her cakes designs and articles have been featured in various sugar art magazines like Cake Masters, Fond bites, Sugar, etc. and in international blogs and forums.

Her achievements are merely because of her love for baking. Though she has been suffering from slip discs for a couple of years, yet her love and passion for baking has triggered and inspired her to look forward. We do believe that health is wealth but your passion and love for things makes you work for the goal. She too works on the same motto that if you love what you are doing, only then you can succeed in it.

Mistakes are proof that you are trying

Failure is not the opposite of success but it is a part of success. An individual is successful if he or she embraces failures and mistakes as teachers. Over a period of the last six years Megha has also come across various such incidents and has drawn great learnings from it. She admits that during this time she has done goof up with recipes, made mistakes in cake designs and structures and found some cakes getting damaged due to weather conditions, many a times faced time mismanagement, packaging and delivery related issues. But she never got bogged down due to such failures. Rather she emerged much stronger and better organized to ensure that she does not repeat such mistakes in the future. All these failures in the past have made her a much better cake artist today. As a result, today she follows a defined flowchart and process for every order she caters.

Since Baking profession involves a lot of creativity and experiments with new ideas, structures, flavors, etc. bakers tend to make some mistakes. It is not how we make mistakes, but how we correct them define us. Being creative all the time is the most challenging but important attribute if you want to succeed in this profession. Each and every designer cake order that she undertakes needs to be customized as per the requirement of the client. So, it's very important to keep herself updated with the current trends and offer new design every time for the clients.

Good things come to those who bake

India has huge potential and opportunity for the home bakers. Not just in Metro cities but even in small towns as well there is great demand for the home bakers. Due to high-speed internet and smartphones available across India, it has become easy to showcase your work and target potential clients. Since online classes can be done from any location so even home bakers have access to the latest techniques and skills which can help them to take their work to the next level. India is still at a nascent stage and the future of home bakers across India looks very promising.

Rabdy Pausch, an American educator, a professor of computer science, human-computer interaction and design has quoted in his book, The last Lecture "We cannot change the cards we are dealt, just how we play the hand."

Mrs. Megha also holds the same opinion and states that we all are blessed with unique skills and intelligence. So introspect into yourself, learn to find your own forte and try to excel in that. Some home bakers have expertise in cream cakes while others can do outstanding work in fondant cakes. Someone can be good at making cute figurines while the other person can be good at making realistic sugar flowers. Home bakers need to choose which domain they should focus on and then channelize their energies and efforts in that direction. Apart from baking, putting efforts on social media pages and making them as attractive as possible is also fruitful as at the first glance, clients will get attracted to the visual appeal only. To increase the sustainability of the client with repeat orders, always use high quality ingredients to get the best taste of your baked goods. Last but not the least she advises newbies to follow their own path and try not to imitate anyone.

Compliments from Clients:

"I wanted to thank you bounds for the amazing cake you gave us. It was very very appealing and appetizing. Everyone was spellbound with the beauty of the cake including us. Thank you so much for bringing the brightest smile on my child's face."

"I attended the anti-gravity class conducted by Megha at her studio recently. Apart from the main topic that was beautifully taught, the tricks and tips that Megha shared were priceless. Looking forward to more such enriching sessions."

"This time i tried my hands on completely fondant cake ♥ Thank u Megha Kwatra Madan it won't be possible without your guidance ♥ n arranging this online class ..each n everything explained so well in detail that I dont even have to ping once to mam for any doubts.. thank u once again mam"

Train your Brain

There has been tremendous change in the mode of learning in the last few years. Many award-winning Indian as well as International Artists are taking classes across India. Due to COVID-19 pandemic these physical classes have been replaced with the online classes and can be attended from the comfort of your home and most of them can be watched again as per your convenient time. Many platforms are organizing collaborations where one can showcase his or her art form. Home bakers should make use of such opportunities and upgrade their knowledge and skills. Always learn from a recognized tutor/ institute who is an expert in their field.

"Baking's meant to be done at home. It's meant to be a good time. It's not about, like, hoarding secrets. It's about sharing them." - Christina Tosi

Mrs. Megha is also well known for hosting platforms where she voluntarily invites International Artists to have live or recorded sessions for training aspiring home bakers in India. She herself has conducted many tutorials and workshops to share her recipes and tips and tricks of baking. If you are passionate about baking and aspire to become professional in the same line, just get in touch with Megha.

Contact Details : +91 98917 97203

Facebook page: https://www.facebook.com/Cakeoluv

Instagram page: https://www.instagram.com/megha_kwatra_madan

Aspiring Baker:

Amolika Khatri - One woman army

"The most beautiful makeup of a woman is passion. But cosmetics are easier to buy" - Yves Saint-Laurent.

Hailing from the land of "Butter Chicken" and "Balle Balle", having resided in different countries, Amolika had paved her way to Baking Industry and is a very popular home baker in Gurugram. She started her home baking business after nine years of her marriage when she had two kids - eight and two years. After completing her MBA degree in HR and Marketing, she joined as an officer in Karur Vysya Bank and worked there for two years. She abandoned her Banking Job after the birth of her beautiful daughter in December 2009 followed by her husband's postings in Singapore and Dubai.

Right from 2009 to 2017, she was a stay-at-home Mom and took full care of her hard-working husband and kids. She utilized all this time in enhancing her cooking skills being very passionate about cooking, experimenting with a variety of recipes and cuisines for her growing children vis-à-vis food-loving husband. All dishes won't come out best in the first try. Her husband who is also her best critic motivated her to keep the passion going. During the flow of cooking and trying new recipes, she happened to try her hands-on baking. Though she baked her first cake in the year 2011, it became a routine for her family.

In 2015, the family shifted to Gurugram from Dubai to have their second baby. Since the ideal family gets completed, she had free mind to explore freely and try to bake exemplary birthday cakes for her own family and near and dear ones.

The Disastrous Birthday Party blossomed a new Baker!!

In her interview with us she revealed that it was a horrible experience with the Birthday cake that they ordered from a renowned bakery of Gurugram for her daughter's 7th Birthday. Like every parent, they too planned for a perfect Birthday party. The cake was designed to match the Birthday dress of their beloved daughter, but what was delivered was a shock for them as design was nowhere what they thought and in addition to that taste was so bad. They felt so embarrassed in front of their guests as the whole portion of cake was untouched. For any Birthday or Wedding party, cake is always the main attraction and if the highlight of the party is not good, the party is ruined.

It is then when she decided that no more cakes to be ordered from outside. Whatever comes in her way, she has to become 'Atam-Nirbhar' and decided to make special events more special not only in our lives but others too.

After that moment she started baking regularly, learned a few icing techniques from YouTube and other internet resources. After four months, she baked an anti-gravity cake for her son's second Birthday and got so much appreciation from the guests and her family and friends. That became the key to move ahead and excel in this field more. To take her creativity to another level, she then attended online sessions for sharp edges from another expert Home Baker who is known for her whipped cream skills. Whenever they had any get together or special occasion, her friends used to wait for artistic designs of her cakes. This is when she gained confidence to launch her business and get paid for her efforts.

Launched her business

In the year 2019, she officially launched her business under the name of अMoli's Treats - not for money but to convert her passion to profession. Initially she had a limited menu and delivery was only within society. Once she gained confidence and appreciation from her initial customers, she scaled up her business. Till date she had baked more than 600 cakes. The orders during special occasions like Valentine Day, Mother's Day, Rakhi are huge and she spends sleepless nights working to deliver her best. The most loved cakes are Pineapple cake and Chocolate Truffle Cake.

Marketing her Cakes

Like any other business, home baking is another business which needs to be marketed well. While talking to this aspiring and rising Home baker, she explained that she uses social media to showcase her cakes. Along with word of mouth, WhatsApp, Facebook and Instagram are good platforms for her to get new customers.

Her support System

She considers her family as the best Support system. Her husband usually does home delivery for the cakes. Important factor that keeps her going is the appreciation and motivation from all the customers to whom she has delivered cakes. With God's grace till now no one has ever reported any issue with the taste of the cakes. This may be due to the fact that she puts in a lot of effort, love and passion while baking a cake.

Failure and fixing tale

This is not a regular feature that you succeed in every venture. Everyone has one or the other bad incident or experience, she too had. A two kg Unicorn design cake was baked for a close friend's daughter's Birthday party. As per her nature, she put in all her best efforts to deliver the best of the best and never compromises with the design. Since her family was also invited as a guest of the party, so they reached the venue with the cake. And while handing over the cake to the host, she asked to cross-check the design and other accessories.

Eagerly waiting to see the creativity, the host opened the box. Ah!! But what happened!! Cake was smashed and tilted to one side. Everyone including the baker was shocked and standing with blank faces. No one knew how it happened and whom to blame for. There was no backup plan as no one will ever dream of such blunder things.

But notice her immediate control of emotions, without loss of temper, requested the host to give some time to fix the mess. Luckily she had a base cake of 1 kg ready at her home for another customer to be delivered at midnight. They went back home and decorated the cake that was ready at home with the same design and reached the venue in less than an hour. The host - a good human being continued to otherwise entertain guests till another cake to utmost satisfaction and happiness was received. The Birthday celebrations were done with the same zeal and zest.

So, it reveals her passion, courage, self-control against all odds and unfavorable situations. Thus, a real winner is one who has turned challenges and failures into seeds of opportunity giving birth to innovation and progress.

How COVID-19 pandemic impacted her business?

Just before the lockdown announced by Indian Prime Minister, Mr Narender Modi on March 24, 2020, she went to her hometown (Ludhiana) and got stuck there, as there was curfew in Punjab. So her business was closed for more than one and half months. People were messaging and asking her for cakes and cupcakes as they were so used to the taste of her cakes and also feared ordering from other bakeries, but she couldn't help them.

They finally returned to Gurugram to continue her business - baking for her cake lovers. For Mother's Day she had fifteen orders to deliver, which she prepared single-handedly with all household chores, absolutely no external help and with kids at home.

New challenge coming her way!!

While I was interviewing her, she told us about a new challenge coming her way. They are relocating to a new city and have to start her baking venture from zero. Well this time not from Zero as she has talent and experience, only her customer base is zero. But I feel when you are talented and have passion, you can fall and rise any number of times. We wish her all the good luck to start her baking journey in the new city. May her business flourish more than before. All the Best Amolika from my side and from all the readers!!!

Some compliments from clients :

"A big thanks to Amolika Khatri for the Impromptu Rakhi hamper, the oreo and pan jar, and dry cakes were so yum and fresh that we all finished in no time. We siblings fought over the last piece just like childhood. You made the rakhi so special. Great value and faith for quality. Looking forward to the next order soon."

"Thanks a lot Amolika for the wonderful cake. I had my anniversary a week back but couldn't decide on the cake till the last moment owing to my corona fear and by then Amolika was all booked. But I couldn't stop myself from ordering the much talked about cakes from Amolika, so I decided to get the cake this weekend from her. I gave her the design but since it was a fondant cake we looked at ways of doing it in cream and had to tweak it a bit. The cake was great and tasted heavenly with absolutely well-balanced flavors. Thanks again Amolika, now I know why everyone is so crazy about your cakes, add me to the list of your cake fans."

"Really appreciate your effort in providing us with the wonderful tasty cake on the occasion of our son's birthday. In these times when some wouldn't even want to keep in touch because of the medical condition we are having to bear with, you came forward and made my son's birthday that much happier and special. Thank you so much for your efforts."

Amolika is a true example of the person who converted her passion to profession and is on the way to excel with her dedication and self-determination. She holds the opinion that your close family is the best supporter, so always seek help from your near and dear ones. Look for the ideas and suggestions and try to follow them to shine in your career.

Contact Details: +91 9811921423

Facebook page:

https://www.facebook.com/amolitreats/

Instagram page:

https://www.instagram.com/amolitreats

Payal Jain

Jovial Homemaker to Potential Baker - Solo Entrepreneur

Payal Jain, who graduated in Food Science and Quality Control from Jammu University, mother of two beautiful kids, started her baking venture in 2016, almost 12 years after her wedding. She runs her home baker business under the name of 'Temptations' from Hoshiarpur, a town in Punjab. She is the First woman in her town to start the concept of home baking.

Her fascination for cakes since childhood is a motivation factor for baking all sorts of flavors and fusions. Creating new designs uplifted her creative mind and allowed her to explore a completely new version of herself. She states that serving her family and friends gave her such a satisfying feeling beyond words.

November 2016 - Family is where any story begins.

It was a special day in Payal's life as twelve years back on the same day she embraced motherhood. Like every year, she planned a small get-together for her daughter's twelfth birthday with close family and friends at home. It was not the first time when the Birthday cake and snacks were prepared at home. As a routine, all special days in their family were celebrated with the same set of guests and a variation in food and snacks being served.

After the guests left, everyone was busy discussing the party, the food, and most importantly, the cake. Both her kids explained to her how all their friends are die-hard fans of their mother's cake. Payal was feeling very proud and satisfied that she could bring a smile to everyone's face, and the day and celebration ended on a happy note. The least she expected that this day still had some impressive moments stored in for her.

Her father-in-law, keen observer of everyone's conversation during and after the party, suggested her to start this as a venture from home. Her mother-in-law, her loving husband, and two kids just jumped with joy at this thought. Seeing the family reaction, Payal was in all smiles and lost in her dream world. The whole night just went in anxiety and giving a serious thought if that was possible as no one in the town had ever done that. So the day she delivered her daughter, the idea of a new baby - 'Temptations' was conceived!!

When TEMPTATION knocks, imagination usually answers.

It is said, "No research without action, No action without research." So it was time to research and do a market survey about the pricing of raw and packaging materials and how to explore the availability of the various decorative materials required to present a cake professionally. It was not a one-day job. She continued baking a few more sample cakes, weighed them, and set the prices for her menu that she planned to offer in her startup's first phase. The planning was followed by printing pamphlets at home and packing slices in small boxes, and distributing them in her neighborhood. To her utter surprise, her colony friends were so amazed by the thought and to encourage and boost her morale, few of them placed the order.

Though for a few months, she used to get nervous about how new clients would react to her bakes because she was using her age-old mother's recipe, which she feared was quite different in taste and texture and is not available in regular bakeries. As time passed, her recipes were accepted wholeheartedly by one and all, and soon a word started spreading mouth-to-mouth. She is very thankful to God and all the driving angels, which kept her spirits high, and she is just loving the way she is climbing the stairs of success and fame.

Giving is the greatest act of Grace.

As per Winston Churchill, "We make a living by what we get, but we make a life by what we give." She frequently put-up stalls for charity with the Red Cross. Many people order cakes from her as Prasad in Temples and churches on various religious occasions like Janmashtami, Hanuman Jayanti, Christmas, and a gesture of thanks and to feed all the devotees there, she adds in a generous amount of cake from her side. Apart from that, she never leaves any opportunity behind to treat her household help and her husband's factory staff on their memorable days. She considers herself contented within her shell, and the feeling is nothing less than any reward.

No Journey is easy

Since she resides in a town, it took a lot of time to introduce the concept of placing the order a couple of days prior because people were so used to walking in the bakery and picking up the stuff. So this was and is still quite a big task. She has been successful to some extent as now most of her clients are aware that they need to order a cake from her beforehand.

The next challenge she faces is procuring the decorative good quality material and stocking for the future as few articles are not available locally in the town, so she had to order online well in time. A couple of times, she had to rethink or create motifs on the spot due to raw materials' unavailability. She has always positively taken these issues because these little challenges again allow her to explore her creativity.

Payal has come a long way in her baking journey and still has plans to expand more, as for her family is always a priority. Being a compassionate mother, she focuses majorly on the studies of her kids. Along with it, she is making efforts to expand her business.

Although she specializes in all types of designer and theme-based cakes, yet her fruit cakes are always high in demand. Spike in the number of orders is seen on festivals and special days like Valentine's Day, Father's Day, Mother's Day, etc. She claims to cater twenty cakes in a day all be herself. Lately she has amazed her clientele with all trending cakes like rasmalai fusion, cheese cakes, piñata and pull up cakes as these cakes were introduced in the town by her.

Payal Jain is a very talented and artistic home baker who considers baking as a therapeutic effect. She started her home baker journey with the encouragement and support of her family, who always motivated her to explore new things. On behalf of all readers and fans, I wish Payal and her business unit all the best wishes to expand and satisfy people's temptations with the delicious cakes.

Compliments from Clients:

"It is difficult to put into words that how your cakes are. Infact, I'm always short of words. The cakes of temptations are mouth melting, with excellent taste and with super awesome looks. See, I am not going to taste cakes from other bakers now. My kids, my whole family, even my parents have become big fans of yours.!! Relishing!"

"I love everything about Temptations♥ Perfect taste, the most tempting cakes and awesome creativity! Payal, is such a beautiful person inside out and her cakes speak for her! She can very beautifully make any occasion special Thank You so much Temptations♥ Rise n shine Much luv♥ "

"Wow feeling on seeing Temptation cake box as it is accompanied by plastic knife and birthday candles. Theme based, fresh, homemade & egg less cake adds flavor. Fascinating look with a perfect blend of fruit, Icing & other ingredients matches high expectations. Finally, the wonderful taste compels to have it more. I am a regular customer of Temptation cakes and recommend trying at least once....... Rest cake shall speak for itself."

Contact Details: +91 9463306517

Facebook page:

https://www.facebook.com/Temptationspayal

Instagram page:

https://www.instagram.com/temptations_payal

Bonus: Tips and Tricks for Upcoming Bakers

After reading stories about women who have donned many hats and accomplished their goals in different areas of Baking Industry, I am pretty sure that you would be definitely inspired and motivated. It also tells you about the potential of the baking industry. If you are creative and dedicated then you can open up your wings and fly as high as you want. At the fag end of my book, I would like to share few tips and tricks which can be useful for any amateur bakers, or home bakers to take their profession to next level.

While interviewing various home bakers across India, I came to know that the baker's community is very helpful and supportive for each other. The artists, whose stories have been published in previous chapters, did not hesitate to disclose the secrets of their success. So, I take this as an opportunity to share the best advice given by these experts for newbies willing to enter in the baking industry.

"Advice is like snow - the softer it falls, the longer it dwells upon, and the deeper it sinks into the mind" - Samuel Taylor Coleridge

There is no denial of the fact that experience and self-realization is the best teacher. But, still I feel some tips and suggestions from the most successful people will help you in boosting your morale. In this chapter, I have consolidated a few points that you can include in your business plan if you are starting fresh. In case you are already aware of these points, these can act as a checklist. If you are good at baking cakes, these points will help you to become better and also will take away your worries to sell them.

Have Patience – Patience is the key to success. So you learn how to take criticism in a positive way, learn from it and you will definitely get successful in whatever you are doing.

Offer your Best - Do not make customers your Guinea pig. Offer only those products which you are best at. It is perfectly fine if you are starting with just a single flavor of cake but it should be perfect.

Menu - Prepare a menu of the products that you will be offering. It is always better to restrict to a limited menu initially, than just trying new recipes to deliver to customers.

Engaging in Collaborations and Competitions - In many of the previous chapters, the importance of collaborations and competitions has been explained. So to bring out the true artist within you, do participate in collaborations frequently.

Make Video - Gone are the days when cakes used to come in simple square or round shape. Additionally, decorate your cakes with cream and cherries. Make sure that your designer 3D shaped cake is best showcased in a video as only a video can have 360-degree coverage.

Attract Customers - A beautiful picture is worth a thousand words. So, photography is very important for attracting customers. Along with baking, focus on improving photography skills too. Photography helps in tracking your progress.

Key Elements – If you are in the baking industry then your key elements should be TASTE & QUALITY. Both taste and quality go hand in hand. If you have good quality products, taste will come automatically.

Enough Lighting- Lighting plays a significant role while clicking pictures. So always make sure that there is adequate lighting when you are saving your beautiful and artistic cake designs through the lens eye.

Registrations - Get all necessary registrations done before launching your business. If you are into the baking industry which comes under the food category, FSSAI license is a must. Check for other licenses depending upon your county and state.

Start with basics – You must start with the basics first. Do not try and make something very extravagant in the beginning. Once you develop expertise in basic items then move ahead and try new things.

Training – If you are a beginner baker or a home baker then you must take professional training. It will help you improvise in the field a lot. Experts give some good tips which can be used in your business.

Out of Crowd Thinking: Try and think about something which others are not offering. If you have some new flavor/ product to offer, this will help you to gain quite a lot of name.

Best recipes – You can make a list of your best recipes and ask your family and friends to try out and give you genuine reviews about the same.

Avoid Awkward Situations – Do not hesitate in trying out recipes at home. Some material might go to waste in the beginning but later on it will give you much more benefits than what you can even think of. It is much better than getting into awkward situations in front of the client. Always practice well before coming out with the final product.

Knowledge – You should never stop to learn. So, gather as much knowledge as you can. Learning is a never-ending process.

Event Participation - Be a part of various events in and around your society by setting up a stall or as an investment distributing some samples of your products.

Rules - Set your own rules for taking orders and running your business. Make sure to take advance payment from customers, so that the order is confirmed from both ends.

Social Media - Present world is known as the digital world, so why not make your digital presence predominant. Increase your visibility through social media. Facebook, Instagram, WhatsApp are excellent platforms to showcase your talent and help you to increase your orders.

Conclusion

Baking industry is a versatile industry. There is so much to learn that you can't even imagine. You should simply select your expert niche, price your art accordingly and take your business to heights. If you want to increase your sales in the beginning then you can contact the local shops and display your posters, you can give a few products as free samples, and also give free classes. The idea is to "Never give up", keep trying till you achieve what you have thought about.

"Home Bakers have created careers for Home Bakers."

About the Author

Daisy Madaan, a Software Engineer by profession, has a successful professional career and is always known for her dedication and passion to work. After spending fifteen years in the corporate world, she took a break from her high-profile job after the birth of her daughter. Sitting at home she realized that there are many women like her who are confined to home after kids. Their dreams, their passion take a back seat. These things kept haunting her and she started looking for women who have paved their way in entrepreneurship despite all odds.

She is now a woman entrepreneur with a mission to inspire women around her. She took up blogging and digital marketing out of her passion for writing. She is the owner of Facebook group 'Creative Wonder Women'. The group is an ideal space for like-minded creative ladies to showcase their creativity in whatever they do - be it kitchen, quality time with kids, decorating the home or birthday planning, designing, any artistic work, baking, etc. Members of the group enjoy and get inspired by the work of other members. You are most welcome to join her group and get inspired or inspire others by your creativity.

Apart from her technical blogs, she has started her website which will have inspiring stories of women entrepreneurs from all fields. The website 'www.powerinher.com' is planned with womanhood as the muse. To rejoice women and their dedication to make the world a better place - one step at a time.

In this book, she has targeted home bakers as they have made love edible with their passion and dedication. The book brings out a powerful message - believe in your passion. Women are creators and not meant to give up. Her advice to all women is play whatever roles you fall into - mother, sister, wife, daughter, daughter-in-law but remember your own worth. Give wings to your dreams and embrace yourself.

She holds a strong opinion that if you love yourself, only then others will love you!!

You can always connect with her on:

Facebook Page: www.facebook.com/DaisyMadaans
Instagram: www.instagram.com/daisymadaan
LinkedIn: www.linkedin.com/in/daisymadaan
Website: www.powerinher.com

Made in the USA
Monee, IL
07 July 2026